THE COUNTRY LIFE LIBRARY OF ANTIQUES
DECANTERS AND GLASSES

THE COUNTRY LIFE LIBRARY OF ANTIQUES

Decanters and Glasses

Therle Hughes

COUNTRY LIFE BOOKS

Frontispiece
Slender glass decanter by Powell & Sons harnessed in silver and
mother-of-pearl by William Hutton & Sons of London; hallmarked for
1902–3. Victoria and Albert Museum, London.

Published by Country Life Books
and distributed for them by
The Hamlyn Publishing Group Limited
London . New York . Sydney . Toronto
Astronaut House, Feltham, Middlesex, England

First published 1982
ISBN 0 600 30458 2

Set in Monophoto Garamond by
Tameside Filmsetting Ltd,
Ashton-under-Lyne, Lancashire
Printed in England by
Hazell, Watson & Viney Limited,
Aylesbury.

Contents

CHAPTER ONE

Early History

GLASS HAS CAUGHT man's imagination ever since he first found glassy fulgurite where lightning-heat had struck the desert sand. As James Howell marvelled in the early 17th century, it was

a rare kind of knowledge and chemistry to transmit dust and sand (for they are the only main ingredients) to such a diaphanous, pellucid, dainty body as you see a Crystal-Glass is . . . .

Cheap, abundant silica, whether in sandstone, flint or purest silver-sand, remains the basic ingredient for making common glass together with equally workaday soda or potash and a little lime. And we can still wonder at the extraordinary qualities of the resultant translucent, light-reflective 'metal' which can be heated to a viscous state and then shaped, stretched, imperceptibly joined, coloured, reheated in an infinity of ways in response to men's skill and imagination.

Within the confines of my subject, decanters and drinking glasses made through the last three centuries range from superbly engraved and gilded trophies to the commonest little tavern dram glass or joey. But the story of glassmaking began, it now appears, at least as early as 2,000 BC, in Mesopotamia, a few centuries before ancient Egyptians evolved glassy glazes to make their stone beads gleam like jewels.

At first beakers and bottles might be shaped by modelling the hot viscous glass around cores of clay and by c. 1,000 BC they could also be cast in moulds. But then, as now, glassmen must have handled their glowing blobs of hot glass on the ends of iron rods. In c. 100 BC probably some enterprising Syrian, using a hollow rod, found that he could shape lighter, thin-walled vessels by blowing air into the heated glass so that it expanded like a balloon. The shape of a vessel might then be controlled by turning and swinging the hollow globe or by blowing it into a simple open-ended mould. Our table glass has been 'free-blown' or 'blown-moulded' ever

since–challenged only by the 19th century's innovation of pressed glass forced into the mould's shape and pattern by a metal plunger.

The blowing technique transformed glassware from a luxury to everyday usefulness and the spread of the Roman empire meant that the craft was practised wherever there was a demand for glass vessels. By the beginning of the Christian era men were already adept at working their glass with all the manipulative and decorative skills we know today. Improvements have depended mainly upon the greater knowledge of materials and furnace techniques that made England's glasshouses from the late 17th century the envy of the world and have given a unique splendour to collections of English table glass.

Under the Romans several furnaces were at work in Britain. But the first direct evidence of a revival in English glassmaking, including cups, beakers and bottles, is found on the Surrey/Sussex borders around Chiddingfold where a coarse glass was made from the 13th century by glassmen from Normandy. This depended on natural deposits of suitable sand and the local timber to heat primitive furnaces. The same woodland provided the bracken, fern and beechwood required for their potash alkali, giving the glass its characteristic greenish tone.

Venice, meanwhile, at the heart of far-reaching trade routes, was certainly making glass again by the 11th century and the renaissance

1. (*Left*) A very fine suite of decanter and glasses, *c.* 1760s, decorated in white enamel with fruiting vines and a SHERRY label. The glasses with compound twist stems – corkscrew ribbons and 'gauze' in white enamel.

2. (*Right*) Goblet of soda glass by Giacomo Verzelini probably engraved in diamond point by Anthony de Lysle. The upper part decorated with stag, unicorn and two hounds among trees, with the date 1578 and initials AT and RT below. The stem with a large melon-shaped knop on a conical foot.

of the arts in the 15th century was reflected in the exquisite vessels created in great secrecy on the island of Murano in the Venice lagoon. Glass of the *façon de Venise* became known in all the courts of Europe for ornate fantastic shapes cleverly manipulated by pincering and trailing. When Henry VIII died in 1547 his 'glass house' at Westminster contained hundreds of pieces of Venetian glass, many proudly mounted in gilded silver.

It was understandable therefore that high quality table glass in the Venetian manner was proposed when a merchant, Jean Carré of Antwerp, obtained a privilege from Elizabeth I in 1567 and, according to the late E. Barrington Haynes, 'established modern glassmaking in England', aided by technicians from Venice. But in the Wealden glassmaking region his fellow Huguenots from Lorraine, mainly intent on making window and bottle glass, came into conflict with the established Normandy men and with local ironfounders, all requiring woodland fuel.

Wood was forbidden to these glassmakers by a proclamation of 1615, but it seems probable that many were already aware of the advantages of burning coal in a new style of furnace. Some moved to the Forest of Dean, others to North Staffordshire and others, notably, to villages around Stourbridge in the West Midlands and to Newcastle upon Tyne. Anglicised forms of these wanderers' names, including Hennezel, Thisac, Thietry and Houx,

3. (*Above*) Tall glasses each flashed with two different colours, with cut stems and decorated bowls, *c.* 1900. Royal Brierley Crystal, Brierley Hill.

4. (*Below*) A range of typical Victorian ingenuity, mid to late nineteenth century. Broadfield House Glass Museum, Kingswinford.

were lastingly associated with Stourbridge and Newcastle glass. The Stourbridge area could offer not only coal, but also high quality fireclay for the glassman's melting pots; Newcastle possessed good materials for furnace-lining.

Carré himself in 1570 set up a glasshouse in London at Crutched Friars, Aldgate, but died in 1572; it was the Venetian expert he had engaged from Antwerp, Jacob Verzelini, who in 1575 was permitted by Queen Elizabeth to make glasses in the Venetian style for twenty-one years. Only nine vessels exist, however, that can be claimed with any probability to be of his manufacture, the light soda-glass showing a greyish-green, smoky-grey or brownish tone, clouded with innumerable tiny bubbles that are masked by the elaborate engraving in diamond-point ascribed to a Frenchman, Anthony de Lysle. Some bear dates between the late 1570s and 1590.

Verzelini retired in 1592, his glasshouse being acquired by financier Sir Jerome Bowes with a twelve-year monopoly and permission to import 'Venetian glass for noblemen'. This source of royal income was continued by James I, the most conspicuous result being that by the 1620s Vice-Admiral Sir Robert Mansell, MP, had complete control of glassmaking throughout the country — drinking glasses, wine bottles, window glass, looking glasses. By then there were glasshouses at Broad Street, Lambeth and Greenwich in the London area and others in or near Stourbridge, Newcastle, Kings Lynn (where he was MP), Swansea, Milford Haven, Wemyss in Fifeshire, Newnham-on-Severn (forerunner of the Bristol glass centre), Barnsley in Yorkshire and many more, covering a work force of about 4,000, as he told Parliament in 1624.

Early 17th-century glassmen were still known in England as Venetians, but by then were strongly influenced by Netherlands work so that it is impossible to distinguish English vessels from various Continental imports in similar lightweight, lustreless glass.

Distribution of Mansell's glass was equally important and in 1635 Charles I granted a charter to the Glass-Sellers' Company which became a powerful body in the 1660s. At this time John Greene, a member of the Company, when ordering table glass from Venice, drew up hundreds of designs showing the sturdy yet elegant vessels then required by his English customers. E. M. Elville has noted that this merchant alone imported some 2,000

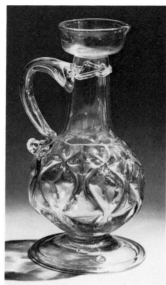

5. (*Left*) Late-16th or early-17th-century flask reputedly found in Oxford, showing how the glass-blower could twist his hot vessel in a swirling pattern that would give it greater strength and a little heat insulation; height 4⅜ ins. Victoria and Albert Museum, London.

6. (*Right*) Small English soda-lime glass wine jug with body ornament and trailing around the neck; the wide mouth intended to aid decanting from the wine bottle, 1660s. Pilkington Glass Museum, St Helens.

dozen glasses between 1667 and 1672. But it was in vain that he stressed his need for 'verrij Bright cleer whit sound Metall' and the Company decided to seek instead to influence improvements in English manufacture.

Interestingly this coincided with similar action in Germany and Bohemia whose hard, clear glass was lustreless, but excellent for the engraved ornament that thereupon became vastly important. In England experiments financed by the Glass-Sellers' Company and leading scientists enabled another prosperous merchant in the Venetian trade to open a glasshouse in the Savoy, London in 1673. This was George Ravenscroft, 1618–81, and what he triumphantly produced was the glass known for a couple of centuries as flint-glass, only within the last century coming to be known as lead crystal.

CHAPTER TWO

The Arrival of Flint-Glass

CHARLES II and his court returned from exile primed in the latest Continental extravagances. But behind their artificial flamboyance many shared an urge to develop native materials and skills that would furnish their surroundings with a new elegance and refinement, even in the presentation of food and drink. Ravenscroft was chosen by the Glass-Sellers' Company for his experience in the Venetian glass trade and also because he was closely associated with the great minds of the day such as Newton, Wren and Samuel Morland.

Surprisingly, within a few months of launching his small glasshouse in the Savoy he announced to the Glass-Sellers' Company that he had achieved a 'fine crystalline glass in semblance of rock crystal for beer, wine and other uses'. He called his glass 'flint crystalline' and the name flint-glass remained but this may be confusing. There was nothing new in his choice of crushed and calcined flint pebbles, rather than the glassman's customary impure sand. These were a common source of silica but in any case were costly to prepare and seldom used after c. 1730, suitable sand being obtained instead from the Isle of Wight (Alum Bay), the Lyn river and Aylesbury.

A patent was granted to him, but his hopes were quickly dashed as this early ware soon lost its transparency, developing a mass of fine interior cracks, a fault known to collectors as crizzling. Not until late in 1675 did he produce the splendid glass now associated with his name—heavy, with a dark, shadowy gleam and a density and refractive brilliance previously unimagined. This glass delights us too with its sonorous ring, a distinctive feature noted by the Glass-Sellers' Company who boasted that no one could be deceived with dull-toned soda or potash glass—although Derek C. Davis has observed that some modern non-lead glass also rings when tapped.

7. A new delicacy in drinking-glass stems was introduced with closely twisted spirals of air or coloured enamel, 1760s. Broadfield House Glass Museum, Kingswinford.

To overcome the fault in his early flint-glass Ravenscroft reduced its proportion of potash alkali; whereas the Germans at this time were experimenting with additional lime he introduced oxide of lead (litharge). This was a technical triumph rather than an invention, for a Florentine treatise on glass *L'arte Vetraria*, 1612, by Antonio Neri had been translated into English by Christopher Merret in 1662 and Chapter 64 of that book referred to 'glass of lead, known to few' as the finest and noblest of glass.

Some of Ravenscroft's glass has been identified, marked with a small seal or glass disc impressed with a raven's head, as borne on his family coat of arms. At the Victoria and Albert Museum a substantial drinking glass in the shape known as a roemer, shows a clear impression of this seal among the strawberry prunts (tooled glass discs) that dot its massive stem. Other makers of fine-quality glass soon introduced their own seals such as the king's arms used by Henry Holden, glassmaker to the king from 1683 with a factory

8. Horseshoe spirit decanter (left) with fox's mask stopper, enamelled huntsman and hounds, decorated by Will Capewell, c. 1935; height 9 ins. 'Enclosure' goblet enamelled by Capewell with figure of fox in stem. Royal Brierley Crystal, Brierley Hill.

in Wapping. Bernard Hughes has noted that flint-glass was quickly in widespread use although it cost about five times as much as the common glass known as 'ordinary glass' or crystal. The glassware was customarily sold by weight and lead-glass was unavoidably heavy.

Some noble drinking glasses remain from this stimulating period. One in the Brooklyn Museum still possesses its lid with an ornate crown finial and strawberry prunts as well as pincered trellis work and the threads of glass across the surface known as trailing. In the Venetian tradition too, its stem is composed of two hollow-blown swellings.

Ravenscroft died in 1681, being succeeded by Hawley Bishopp. His death coincided with expiry of his patent and soon many flint-glass houses were at work, making fine table ware. Much of this was exported, for comparable Continental flint-glass dates no earlier than the St Cloud ware of the 1780s.

9. (*Left*) English version of the roemer, made in flint-glass. Among the prunts on the hollow stem is the seal (raven's head in relief) used by George Ravenscroft; height 6½ ins, 1678–81. Victoria and Albert Museum, London.

10. (*Right*) Covered goblet ascribed to Ravenscroft's glasshouse, the lid topped by a magnificent crown finial and both lid and body decorated with circuits of prunts, *c.* 1680. Brooklyn Museum, New York.

These early makers of decanters and glasses had many problems, however. There was, for instance, the suggestion of greenish or greyish tint in the glass—a tinge rather than a colour, but distinctly darker than clear modern glass, due to impurities in their ingredients. These long prevented production of a completely colourless glass, despite the addition of such decolourisers as cobalt, manganese and nickel—with somewhat unpredictable results. They were at

16

pains, too, to increase and more exactly control furnace heat and so ensure perfect fusion, avoiding specks and tiny bubbles. Undulations within the glass known as striae or veins proved especially difficult to remove. Most important of all, perhaps, was the development of adequate annealing so that the stresses in a newly made glass vessel could be released under heat followed by slow uniform cooling. Only then could it withstand subsequent sudden changes of temperature.

Early Georgian technical advances included the hotter, more reliable Perrott furnace, patented 1734, which meant that the glass could be heated in larger melting pots. For annealing, the tunnel leer (from *leer ofen*, empty furnace) was designed so that the glass could progress slowly 'from a very intense degree of heat to the temperature of the common air'. George Ensell, descendant of the important Stourbridge Hennezel family, is associated with improvements to this leer in 1780, leading to more adventurous ornamental cutting.

Such an expanding industry proved tempting to the government however. The first *Glass Excise Act* imposing a duty on glass lasted only from 1695 to 1699, but temporarily closed down scores of glasshouses. The Act of 1745 and subsequent still heavier duties were not repealed for 100 years. The charge in 1745 was a penny a pound weight on the glassmakers' raw materials with no allowances for breakages. Much worse was the amendment in 1777 which included even the broken glass (cullet) that formed a considerable portion of the mixture.

Since the tax was calculated on weight rather than value, it became profitable to sell the lightweight vessels decorated with the more elaborate ornament that became technically possible during the 18th century. In any case fashion favoured such a change, to the delight of present-day collectors. Further tax increases followed in 1781 and 1787 and by 1820 the charge had reached 10½d. per pound weight, reduced to 6d. in 1835. Much more than cost was involved: glassmen had to accept the constant presence of officials assessing the duty, to the detriment of experiment and innovation, an uncomfortable state of affairs that ended only with the lifting of the duty in 1845.

It is against such technical considerations that the collector follows the fashion styles in English decanters and drinking glasses.

Trade concessions in the 1713 *Treaty of Utrecht* flooded the country with foreign goods and it is perhaps remarkable that the collector can trace, nevertheless, a native individuality and grace wonderfully well suited to the qualities of English flint-glass. In his hundreds of drawings the importer John Greene had declared the English love of simple, well proportioned, sturdy design and this can be seen in the glassware associated with successive fashions in home furnishings.

By the end of the 17th century, according to John Houghton, FRS, in *Letters for the Improvement of Commerce and Trade*, twenty-seven glasshouses were making flint-glass up and down the country. Nine were in London and others around Stourbridge, Bristol, Newcastle, Leeds, Nottinghamshire, Coventry, Liverpool, King's Lynn, Worcester and Yarmouth.

Trend-setting London included, for example, not only the Savoy flint glasshouse, but others in Lambeth and Whitechapel and the Falcon in Southwark. By 1833, according to an Excise inquiry, only three London flint-glasshouses were at work; only the Whitefriars near the Temple under James Powell and Sons survived into this century, moving to Wealdstone in 1922 after almost continuous activity from 1709.

Among provincial centres the Stourbridge area, including Dudley, Brierley Hill and Wordsley, has continued to be of first importance since glass workers from Lorraine arrived from the Chiddingfold area in *c*. 1612 in search of coal for their furnaces. By the 1750s, according to Dr Richard Pococke in his *Travels Through England*, Stourbridge had become important 'especially for its coloured glass'. Opaque white glass, flower-painted in coloured enamels, was seen then as a potential rival to the new porcelain and white salt-glazed stoneware and R. J. Charleston has suggested a Midlands origin also, rather than Bristol, for the white glass vessels described in Chapter Four.

From *c*. the 1760s shallow cutting of glass also became important. Some especially brilliant engraving, too, is associated with this area in the 19th century when nearby Birmingham also had an important share in Britain's technical brilliance acclaimed at the international exhibitions. In more workaday mood, improved moulds for shaping glass are associated with Stourbridge and the first English experiments with cheap ornament in pressed glass, popular in the

11. Decanter signed *Beilby Jun*ʳ *Pinxit & Inv*ᵗ *N'Castle* – suggesting that the ornament pre-dates the death of Beilby's father in 1765. This is confirmed by a date *1762* added in diamond-point; Victoria and Albert Museum, London.

12. (*Top left*) Shaft-and-globe bottle in purple flint-glass showing the string ring round the neck to secure the cork and the attractive surface patterning described by him as 'nipt diamond-wais'; Height 6¼ ins, *c.* 1675–80. Victoria and Albert Museum, London.

13. (*Top right*) Rummer, *c.* 1801, showing a ship under the Wearmouth Bridge, Sunderland, opened 1796. On the reverse the motif of rose, thistle and shamrock suggests association with the Union of Great Britain and Ireland in 1801. Victoria and Albert Museum, London.

14. (*Above*) Slender-stemmed balustroid glasses ascribed to Newcastle but probably all engraved in Holland, the central vessel attributed to Jacob Sang.

United States, were made by the Richardson firm of Wordsley in 1833 (and probably in Newcastle a few months later). By 1874, when other traditional glass regions were declining, the area had forty-one glasshouses. H. J. Haden in his *Notes* on the Stourbridge trade in 1949 regretted only the passing of such picturesque events as the glass-makers' picnics when they carried 'spectacular examples' of their craftsmanship through the streets.

This love of parading their precious wares was so important that when Prince Frederick and Princess Augusta visited Bristol in 1738 glassmen carrying swords, sceptres and trumpets of glass headed the procession of city dignitaries. John Houghton noted three flint-glass works there in 1696, but eventually the difficulty in obtaining cheap coal probably contributed to the craft's decline in the early 19th century. Like Stourbridge, Bristol was noted for milk-white glass and for cut glass and probably made some of the mid-Georgians' most delightful colour-twist drinking glasses.

In Newcastle in 1823, as recorded by the *Newcastle Journal*, the glassworkers' guild procession had each man wearing a glass feather in his hat, a glass star and coloured drops on his coat, and carrying a staff to display his craft–'decanters, goblets, drinking glasses, jugs, bowls, dishes'–while some rang glass bells.

Some collectors today have a special regard for the drinking glasses, mainly of the 1730s to 1760s, from Newcastle, an area covering Gateshead, South Shields and Sunderland. Coal had been mined there since the 13th century and two flint-glasshouses were at work through much of the 18th century, including the Closegate taken over by a Stourbridge glassmaker in 1731 when John Williams married into the long-established Dagnia glassmaking family from Italy. Vessels especially associated with the region include decanters and drinking goblets painted in enamel by Newcastle's renowned glass decorators William and Mary Beilby, at work *c.* 1762 to 1778. English wheel-engraving can be associated positively with the area when the subject is the famous Wear Bridge recorded on souvenir wares far into Victorian days. But more is known of the region's several 19th-century glassworks associated with the introduction of pressed glass. This thick, heavily ornamented glass became of increasing importance after the abolition of the tax-by-weight in 1845, some items being blessed with makers' marks or design-date symbols.

CHAPTER THREE

Custom and Purpose

GREENE, ORDERING from Venice *c.* 1670, specified glasses for sack, claret, beer, Rhenish, brandy and French wine and illustrated, for example, tumblers for beer, claret and sack, funnel and rounded-funnel bowls on short stems for French wine and the hollow-stemmed German Rhenish roemer. Glass-sellers' advertisements through the following century tirelessly fostered the notion that different drinks required their own peculiar vessels. Collectors today who want to find the intended purposes of their decanters and 'wine glasses' may have to search widely for clues in paintings, trade cards, old catalogues – and accept some inconclusive findings.

Among decanters it is remarkable to note how persistently narrow-mouthed jug shapes, with beak spouts and handles, were offered for the Englishman's favourite claret. Here Ravenscroft's handled decanters followed a style already established in delftware before claret almost disappeared as a result of the *Methuen Treaty* of 1703. This treaty stipulated that the duty on Portuguese wines should be less by one third than that on French. Claret and champagne, for example, then became rare luxuries and those with no palate for the rough Portuguese wines might turn instead to gin and a new quality of strong-ale. Significantly, claret was nevertheless prominent among the names engraved or ostentatiously enamelled on the mid-century's most elegant 'labelled' decanters. Handled jugs for the drink appeared again, though rarely, from the 1770s and more are to be found among deeply cut serving vessels through the 19th century. Goblets – a general term for drinking glasses with a capacity of at least four ounces – were available for drinking claret, their large rounded bowls supported on stems of all the most fashionable patterns. This compared with two to three ounces for wine glasses, three to four ounces for ales. (Today the recommended capacities, to allow for filling the vessels two-thirds, are: 8 oz. for champagne, 6 to 8 oz. for burgundy, 5 oz. for claret, 3 oz. for port and sherry and about 1 oz. for liqueurs.)

15. (*Left*) Champagne glass with double-ogee bowl balanced by a domed foot and a compound opaque twist stem, *c.* 1760–70.

16. (*Right*) Short-stemmed flutes of about the mid 18th century, their purpose indicated by the wheel-engraved ornament of fruiting vine (for champagne) and hop and barley (for strong ale).

Champagne as a semi-sparkling liquor was popularised in the late 17th century by Charles II's French friend, the Chevalier de Saint Evremond, and maintained its reputation for celebratory drinking despite the huge tax on French wines, increased still further in 1763. The early Georgian cruciform decanter ensured thorough cooling when it was placed in iced water in a wine cistern; in the 1750s Thomas Betts in widely quoted advertisements listed 'neat champagne quart decanters'. This refers to a design with a hollow pocket slanting down into the body to hold ice, capped with a cork mounted in silver or Sheffield plate, and still occasionally found among Victorian vessels.

For drinking champagne Saint Evremond recommended tall flutes to minimise evaporation and these are in fashion again today. They may be seen in some happy portrait groups through the 18th century. Fruiting vine engraving may distinguish such vessels from strong-ale flutes engraved with hop and barley. Fashion decreed that the glass should be gill-size, but only half filled; hence the shallow ribbing or fluting often introduced on the lower half of the bowl to add to the liquor's sparkle, this style being described by Betts as 'worm'd [that is on an air-twist stem] and half-ribbed'.

Argument continues, however, concerning the early use of tazza-shaped glasses for champagne, probably introduced when George I came to the throne. Betts advertised half-moulded egg-shaped champagne glasses and this outline accorded well with the moulded pedestal stem also probably introduced by the Hanoverians. But the resultant vessel proved so popular for serving sweetmeats that collectors are most likely to find what is generally assumed to be the sweetmeat holder, with an everted or flared rim.

When champagne was welcomed back after the Napoleonic Wars, flute glasses were widely sold for it. These are now generally known as short ales, listed in 1817, for instance, with button stems, plain stems on goblet (square) feet or with thistle and ring bowls. But the more sparkling drink developed in the late 1820s prompted a return to a hemispherical bowl richly decorated and described by Disraeli in 1832 as 'a saucer of ground glass mounted upon a pedestal of cut glass'. For the connoisseur a tulip shape was noted as 'new fashioned' in 1858.

Flute glasses with tall narrow conical bowls are associated especially with ale, of course – one result of the high tax on French wines being the promotion of highly alcoholic strong-ale as distinct from the cheap frothy nappy ales served in tumblers known as quaffing glasses. Hence the small size of early strong-ale serving jugs. Lady Grisell Baillie in 1715 paid half as much again for ale glasses as for wine glasses, the flute bowls being of thick glass, reducing capacity and obscuring the ale's still-murky appearance. Some in the late 17th century retained the Venetian fashion for added moulding spiralling around the lower part of the bowl.

When strong-ale became a more attractive looking amber liquor in the late 1730s it was drunk from clear glass in tall bowls in all the popular shapes. From the 1740s these were often wheel engraved with the hop and barley motifs found also on some ale jugs. Bees and butterflies here are thought to indicate the long-popular buttered ales, mentioned by Pepys, which included honey. (Nowadays mead, made from fermented honeycomb dregs, is often associated with a stemmed glass that has a cup-shaped bowl, for lack of proof to the contrary, although E. Barrington Haynes suggested 'a goblet with stem rudimentary or absent'.)

Stems followed the fashions of their day, tall, short and dwarf, but few ale vessels were more pleasing than the simplest style with a trumpet bowl drawn smoothly into a short tapering stem on a conical foot. Towards the end of the century rummers, too, were used for ale.

I have referred above to the popularity of dwarf and short ale flutes among champagne drinkers and others in the 1820s. In contrast there was a liking too for the giant ale glass over a foot tall and the so-called yard-of-ale mentioned in the mid 17th century as an ell glass ($1\frac{1}{4}$ yards) for beer. John Evelyn in 1685 recorded the drinking of the king's health in 'a flint glass of a yard long'. In the 18th century the vessel had a ball knop between the flute bowl and the highly domed folded foot, but in the 19th century merely a flat foot, different again from the trick glass popular in the 1830s to 1840s with a hollow bulb at the base. Extremely tall slender flute bowls on simply knopped stems were illustrated by the Edinburgh Glasshouse Company in c. 1815.

Beer tumblers found today are usually the 19th century's broad short vessels, heavy and often richly cut. Handled beer mugs and tankards may be found. One of c. 1725 in the Victoria and Albert Museum is a faithful reproduction of the silver or pewter vessel, with strengthening bands around rim, middle and spreading base. Later specimens range from the slightly waisted late-18th-century vessel with heavy reeding above a substantial foot, ensuring stability, to closely patterned vessels of Victorian pressed glass and the general run of cheap tavern wares.

Tall flutes have been associated, too, with cider drinking ever since the first Lord Scudamore recommended them for his finely blended and bottled liquor. But the most easily recognised cider vessels are the mid-18th-century labelled decanter and the glass with a rounded-funnel, ogee- or bucket-shaped bowl engraved with apple trees or perhaps a codlin moth. (Engraved pear sprigs might decorate glasses for the drink made from pears called perry.) These were intended for bottled cider, given fashion status in the 1750s to 1760s despite the imposition of a tax in 1763. Glasses may be found with the slogan NO EXCISE, pre-dating 1766 when the tax was modified. Reduced wine imports at the century end boosted cider sales again and some fine tall Regency flutes are to be found richly engraved and on twisted stems.

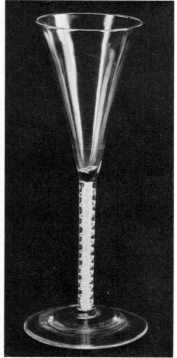

17. (*Opposite top left*) Cider glass with bucket bowl engraved with a fruiting apple tree. There is a codlin moth (enemy of apple growers) on the reverse. With a substantial air-twist stem.

18. (*Opposite top right*) Toasting glass with delicately twist-patterned stem, *c.* 1750. Victoria and Albert Museum, London.

19. (*Opposite bottom*) Small-bowled cordials among a group of glasses with, centre front, a so-called ratafia glass, perhaps for brandy-surfeit water.

20. (*Above*) Decanters for colourless liquors. Left: glass stained with colour and wheel-engraved. Centre and right: clear glass thickly cased with colour. Rounded 'peephole' facets cut through to the clear glass produce diminished views of similar facets on the other side of the vessel. Broadfield House Glass Museum, Kingswinford.

Quite the prettiest 18th-century wheel-engraving was reserved for the decanters and glasses associated with the highly alcoholic aromatic compounds or cordials made from fermented fruit juices, the equivalent of modern liqueurs. Doubtless these were sipped from the early 18th century's knop-stemmed glasses known as light balusters and balustroids with small funnel and bell-shaped bowls rendered even less capacious by their thick bases so that they would hold perhaps an ounce of the potent drink.

Such tiny bowls on tall slender stems might be considered effeminate enough, but cordial glasses came into their own when early-Georgian hostesses served cordials with the tea that ladies enjoyed in the drawing room after four o'clock dinner while their menfolk lingered over their wines. *The Female Spectator* in 1744 made the remarkable comment that excessive tea drinking caused a dejection of spirits necessitating recourse to more animating liquors and

the bottle and the cordial glass are as sure an appendix to the tea table as the slop basin. Brandy, rum and cordials are the usual accompaniment to tea.

In fashionable society the bottle might be replaced by a shapely little decanter wheel-engraved or painted in enamels: pint-sized cordial decanters were advertised in 1744. But the most charming feature of the ritual was the decoration on the cordial glasses themselves. They were listed at the time as flowered glasses and the ornament, wheel-engraved or white-enamelled around their ogee or other roundish bowls, harmonised charmingly with the newly fashionable porcelain teaware. Often there was colour too in their enamel-twist stems, until all this rococo gaiety gave place to the sparkle of all-over facet-cutting attuned to the candle-bright indoor evening social festivities of fashion in the reign of George III.

Sophie von la Roche in her *Diary* noted small cordial decanters in 1786, when the slender facet-cut vessel might be mounted on a square pedestal foot. A little later another diarist Joseph Farrington noted a Scottish hostess serving her guests to 'small glasses of cherry brandy, lemon brandy etc.' from a case of cordials set before her.

It may be mentioned here that a pint decanter was a 'half-bottle' size; quarter-bottle and 'baby' sizes were made too. But more

interesting names were given to the larger vessels: Nebuchad-
nezzar for a 20-bottle capacity, Balthasor for the 16-bottle, Sal-
manazar for the 12-bottle, Methuselah for the 8-bottle, Rehoboam
for the 6-bottle, Jeroboam for the 4-bottle and magnum for the
2-bottle size. The decorative liqueur set–decanter and six glasses
on a tray–survived of course into this century, with René Lalique,
for example, contributing suitably small elegant designs between
wars, decorated on stopper finial and stem with his popular dancing
figures.

By the 1790s a now rare alternative was a decanter with a bulbous
body divided into four vertical sections, each with a stoppered
mouth, to contain half-pints of four different cordials–eight
cordials to the customary pair of decanters. But by then the vogue
for cordials was waning.

Among cordial glasses, the most richly decorated at this time
was the occasional vessel of similar height but with a contrasting
bowl shaped as an extremely long narrow flute. Collectors often
call this a ratafia glass for a brandy infusion including almond
kernels and soft fruits, suited, one would think, to the usual cordial
glass. A more likely explanation, substantiated by Bernard Hughes,
was that these glasses were made readily distinguishable because
they offered the potent medicinal brandy-surfeit-water, decora-
tively presented, but intended to help the heavy drinker through
the mid-century's formidable festivities.

A glass of cordial might be called a dram but this term is more
often associated with a very different class of liquor, the cheap gin
that caused appalling havoc among the poor through early Georgian days despite the ban half-heartedly imposed by the *Gin Act* of
1736. In the 17th century strong waters–distilled spirits such as
gin, whisky and rum–might be drammed or swallowed at a gulp
from small thimble-shaped dram cups. In early flint-glass, gin
drams or nips might have narrow trumpet bowls on short thick
stems and wide heavy feet, sometimes domed, terraced or radially
moulded. Gin glasses used in fashionable circles followed current
styles of stem, but far more remain of the workaday little vessels
three or four inches tall, including the firing glasses mentioned
among commemoratives (Chapter Thirteen).

Collectors sometimes refer to drams as Hogarth glasses, as seen
in such pictures as *The Rake's Progress*, but the style continued to be

21. (*Left*) Toastmaster's glass, its funnel-shaped bowl so thick that it contains a minimal amount of liquor. With a short knopped stem on a plain foot, *c.* 1730. Victoria and Albert Museum, London.

22. (*Right*) Toddy lifter with strawberry diamond cutting and engraved with a crowned Garter and the initial s; made for Augustus Frederick, Duke of Sussex. Victoria and Albert Museum, London.

plentiful throughout the century with thick bowls on short drawn stems and with feet often still showing rough pontil marks even into Victorian days. Some were stemless and another alternative was the cheap little waisted tumbler two or three inches tall with thick ribbing around the base made in abundance for perhaps a hundred years from *c.* 1750. The double-bowled dram glass from the 18th century is found occasionally, the bowls linked directly by their bases or by a short straight stem. Their most obvious purpose was to hold different quantities of liquor (single and double measure).

23. Spirit decanter of the late 18th or early 19th century showing the period's formal style of gilded 'label'. Hollands was the fashionable name for gin. Victoria and Albert Museum, London.

Sham drams were cheap tavern versions of the glass with a deceptively shallow bowl holding perhaps half an ounce required by the man who had to officiate soberly as a toastmaster. The term toasting itself harks back to those rough Portuguese wines of the 1700s which might be made more palatable with spiced toast, although champagne was preferred, of course, for the period's new fashion for toasting the ladies. For a short time this ritual called for a peculiarly delicate flute glass with a stem perhaps one-eighth inch across to be snapped when a precious toast had been drunk. Surprisingly some are still found today.

Glass squares for serving spirits appear to have been made from the 1720s and well suited the late 18th century's fine cabinet-makers' travelling cases and the Victorians' tantalus frame. Sets of blue glass decanters and squares may show gilded 'labels' for hollands (gin), rum and brandy; typically these have the initials H, R and B on their stoppers as it was important for the stopper to be returned to its own decanter, being individually ground for a perfect fit. A fourth decanter might be included for the mixture of spirit, sugar and fruit juice known as shrub.

Curiously enough one of the more confusing terms for the beginner is the rummer. A vessel now usually distinguished by the spelling roemer was ordered by Greene from Venice as a Rhenish and made in flint-glass by Ravenscroft. A fine sealed example is in the Victoria and Albert Museum illustrated in Chapter Two. This has a nearly spherical bowl and a broad hollow sediment-collecting stem made easy to grasp by small raised blobs of glass known as prunts. This was a 'rummer' to the Glass-Sellers' Company; it resembled a German vessel in green glass made not for rum but for hock. Very soon the English version had a solid prunted stem. It is to be found again in glasshouse pattern books of the early 19th century.

Meanwhile in 1730 Bailey's dictionary defined a rummer merely as a large drinking vessel and as 'such a one fill'd up to the brim'. They are found in a wide range of sizes but most often holding about half a pint and it is clear that the goblets now generally called rummers were used for beer or any of the 18th and 19th centuries' water-diluted drinks, such as lemonade and fashionable punch. The typical style from c. the 1760s was a deep ovoid bowl tapering into a brief drawn stem on a substantial foot. From c. 1790 they

24. Typical hob-nobs of the early 19th century. The example on the right is in dark, heavily leaded glass.

were made as three-piece glasses, but still with all the decorative interest concentrated on bowl and foot.

They are avidly collected for their engraving, of course, but this seldom offers clues as to their original use, save for an occasional hop and barley to suggest mulled ale. But in the 1780s the vessel became associated with the new fashion for hot toddy – rum-and-water 'grog' with lemon, sugar and nutmeg. (Scots made whisky toddy.) Hot rum punch, toddy and other spicy drinks were sipped from the strongly based rummers of cheap glass often called hob-nobs when associated with the quiet fireside companionship known as hob-nobbing. Of special interest to the collector is the occasional massive rummer 10 or 12 inches tall, holding $1\frac{1}{2}$ pints or more, used for preparing the drink.

A wide shallow punch bowl required a ladle, whereas toddy from the giant goblet could be served more safely with a toddy lifter, an elegant little tool on the pipette principle derived from the silver valinch used by the vintner for dipping wine from a cask. In shape it resembles a small slender decanter, but with an entrance at each end. The user plunged the body vertically into the liquor and when it had filled he created a vacuum by placing a thumb over the hole at the top, removing it again to release the toddy into his glass.

Another group of vessels (illustrated in Chapter Two) is associated with the hot spicy drinks of posset and caudle favoured down the centuries as invalids' drinks especially after childbirth. In early Georgian days the curdled spicy wine might be enriched with cream or eggs and oatmeal; as made by Ravenscroft the young mother's lidded two-handled 'invalid cup' had a spout low in the body to ensure that she drank the most nourishing part of the concoction. Seemingly, she often had to share it when the drinking of her health in caudle became a popular ritual for congratulatory visitors through the 18th century. Two fine examples from the 1670s to 1680s are in the Fitzwilliam Museum, Cambridge.

Other minor special-purpose glasses are the vessels now generally called stirrup cups or coaching glasses that consist only of bowl and stem so that they must be held until emptied. Obviously the design would be favoured by innkeepers who had to bring drinks out-of-doors to serve somewhat elusive customers involved in coach stages, hunt meets and the like. The design prompted them to drink up and return the glass safely without delay. However, some vessels found today appear too well finished for this purpose, the bowl perhaps cut with minor ornament below the rim and with fluting above a knopped stem that ends in a faceted ball. Doubtless many of these originally fitted into compartmented travelling cases along with the square decanters that I describe in Chapter Seven, many coach passengers preferring to carry their own provisions.

Sets of musical drinking glasses are among the collector's odder byways, invented by an Irishman, Richard Pockrich, 1690–1759. These were played by running a wetted finger round the rims, the vessels being 'tuned' by adjusting their water content. The notion delighted London society, inspired Mozart to compose a quintet and prompted the many-sided Benjamin Franklin to devise an improved 'glass armonica'. Sets of musical glasses were still being made in the 19th century, more exactly tuned in the course of manufacture.

CHAPTER FOUR

Manufacture

MOVEMENT, controlled, orderly but unceasing, seems to fill the glass-makers' workshop, men and youths going about their tasks at a pace set by that astonishing material–the glass itself. Glass surely is among the most magical of craftsman materials. When hot the glowing viscous blob can be inflated like a bubble, with any surface patterning enlarged, but not distorted; it can be spun into cobweb threads; cut with shears and joined again invisibly; built up in layers of different colours, so that the glass fuses imperceptibly but the colours remain entirely distinct, no matter how thinly it is blown or how fantastically it is shaped and twisted. Near magic indeed, and like magic all too easily shattered into nothingness.

The pace set by flint-glass is more exacting than with more fluid ductile soda-glass and even the lighting is dictated by the need to determine precisely the heat indicated by its colour. Hence the spectacular effect of hurrying youths carrying hot glowing glass between furnace-opening and work bench, the glass gathered on iron rods dipped into the melting pots inside the furnace and twisted for each 'gather' like treacle round a spoon. Hence, too, the ceaseless movement of the men who make up a team or chair.

The gaffer, the man in charge of the whole operation, sits on his 'chair', a bench with flat arms so that at every stage the hot glass, attached to a metal rod, can be rolled to and fro to maintain its symmetry. The whole process has changed little since it was des-cribed in 1751 in the *Universal Dictionary of Arts and Sciences*, although it varies a little in different glasshouses. The glass-blower takes the viscous glass on a long metal blowpipe, rolling it on a flat marver of polished steel (once a slab of marble), to give it pre-liminary shaping as he inflates it by blowing down the pipe, and then swings and tools the hollow bulb. If a drinking glass is being made its stem may be drawn out of the base of the blown bowl (an early style known as a straw-shank glass), but often the stem is shaped separately (stuck-shank). As the seated gaffer rolls the

25. Glass blower at work, seated at his 'chair'. Note the flat arms of
the 'chair', enabling the hot glass to be rolled to and fro.
Cumbria Crystal.

blowing rod on the chair arms, to keep the bowl symmetrical, his
chief assistant or servitor must add more hot glass, rolled and
shaped into the stem, with yet more glass flattened by the second
assistant or footmaker into the foot, and for each process the glass
must be reheated whenever necessary to retain its plasticity at a
subsidiary furnace 'glory hole'.

Every collector knows the term pontil or ponty for the iron rod
attached to the base of the vessel's foot for the later stages of its
making. This rod holds the vessel while the gaffer quickly detaches
the inflated bowl from the metal blow pipe (by localised chilling

such as with a wet tool). Again the hot vessel is kept in shape by the gaffer rolling the pontil rod on the chair arms while trimming the bowl edges with shears (his tool perhaps leaving a very slight irregularity where it last touches the rim) and perfecting the shape with spring-tongs before a junior assistant or taker-in hurries it away to the slow stress-releasing processes of the annealing furnace.

D. C. Davis in *English and Irish Antique Glass* suggests that the faint marks near the top of the bowl that used to be left by the tooling are the most difficult for the faker to reproduce. But such marks could be avoided when the old steel spring-tongs or 'pucellas' were given wooden tips.

In the old days the pontil was attached to the vessel's base by a small knob or seal of hot glass and when this was snapped off it left a tiny twisted scar. This was an expected detail on the concave base of a drinking glass made earlier than *c.* 1780 and continued on cheap vessels long after good quality work showed merely the smooth hollow where it had been polished away (and inevitably was introduced conspicuously on many crudely made fakes). But Victorian glassmen *c.* 1860 devised a rod with a spring-operated grip to fit the glass foot, known as a gadget. This left no scar and meant that glasses could be made with feet that were more or less flat – but less shapely in consequence.

Ornament on a free-blown glass may be cut or engraved or coloured as described in the next chapter, but sometimes a vessel's surface shows a gentle rippling pattern discernable to the finger both inside and outside the bowl. This indicates that the blower has forced the soft gathering of hot glass into a part-size surface-patterned metal mould before enlarging it by further blowing. Simple mould-blown patterns such as vertical ridges are to be found on early flint-glass vessels, the mould often providing the base for a twisted or tooled ornament such as the spiral ribbing described as wrythen in old records. For 'purling', which suggests gadrooning around the base of a drinking-glass bowl, the partly inflated bowl received an extra gather of glass which was shaped in a shallow fluted mould. The lower body of a decanter could be given form as well as ornament when the glass was blown into a shallow mould.

Obviously the mould had to be designed so that the drinking-glass bowl or decanter base could be lifted out of it. But from 1802

26. (*Left*) Bohemian-style decoration greatly admired by mid-19th-century Victorians. 27. (*Right*) Typically shaped early Victorian decanters, the yellow tones well-displayed by the cut ornament. Both from Broadfield House Glass Museum, Kingswinford.

a two-part mould might be used, opening to release the vessel; three-part moulds followed from 1820. This Stourbridge development gave a great boost to the cheaper range of flint-glass tableware, clear and in transparent colours such as blue, amethyst, purple and amber, with surface pattern no longer restricted to the vertical or spiralling ribs that could be withdrawn from a one-piece mould.

Bernard Hughes noted that a writer in *The Queen* in 1902 recorded over 250 patterns for blown-moulded tumblers of brilliant glass, delicately decorated and already then regarded as collectors' items.

Use of this cost-cutting tool might be revealed when the glass

28. Popular opalescent glass. Left: late-19th-century Stourbridge glass.
Centre: clear glass cased with ruby. Right: white opaline glass with
enamelled and gilded decoration by the Richardson firm, *c.* 1850.
Broadfield House Glass Museum, Kingswinford.

blown into the mould penetrated the cracks between the mould
sections, creating small raised 'seams' over the vessel's surface. But
seams proved a more serious problem on vessels shaped by pressing. This development from America, patented in 1830, was
promoted by the Richardson firm of Wordsley from 1833, becoming more widely used for table glass from the 1860s.

In pressed-work the hot semi-fluid glass was forced with a metal
plunger into every crevice of the elaborately patterned several-
sectioned mould, inevitably including those between the mould
sections although the resultant seams might be masked by the
pattern detail. Pressed glass can be distinguished from mould-

29. (*Left*) Mould-blown decanters in Irish glass: Left and right: with fluting, milled neck-rings and pinched stoppers. Engraving includes rose, thistle and shamrock with Irish harps and (centre) the date 1783 and flags declaring Liberty and Free Trade (the political changes that enabled the Irish to export their glass).

30. (*Right*) Opaque white glass decanter gilded on neck, body and matching stopper finial. This conforms with some decanters sold by Christies in 1774 from the stock of James Giles, London decorator, described as '. . . glass decanters in stag's heads and pateras, with festoons, husks, etc. . .'

31. (*Below*) White pressed-glass tankard, the pattern registered 1880 by Henry Greener of Sunderland. Victoria and Albert Museum, London.

40

32. Blue glass with finely gilded 'labels' and with correspondingly lettered stopper finials. The two sets are full-size decanters flanking sauce bottles.

blown because the pattern is generally much more clear-cut on the outside of the vessel while the inside is smooth. In good quality pressed glass 'fire polishing' with a hot flame improves the surface to suggest hand-cut work, but cannot give the same smooth clean brightness to deeper recesses of the pattern. Confusingly, however, the pressed or moulded pattern could always be touched up with wheel-cutting. Sometimes a pressed pattern gives itself away by including details so placed that no cutting wheel could reach them.

For solid glass details, such as decanter stoppers, pedestal feet and some drinking glass stems, the glassman might turn to the pinchers, recognised as a separate trade as early as 1777. These men often had their own small tax-dodging furnaces, concentrating on a limited range of items that could be shaped from heated glass rods placed between the patterned dies of their hand-operated pincers.

Colours were introduced into and on to the surface of the glass mainly in metallic oxides – the glassmen of London, Stourbridge and Bristol being renowned for their colours as early as the mid-18th century, when the first favourite was blue prepared from re-fined cobalt. In Bristol, blue glass is associated with the renowned glasshouse active from 1771 to 1806, run by Lazarus Jacobs and his son Isaac. But the popular term Bristol blue probably first indicated a high quality of the refined cobalt oxide rather than the glass itself. This colour was imported from Silesia and hence in short supply in the late 1750s to 1760s owing to the Seven Years' War.

Rich blue glass goblets, rummers and loving cups are associated also with the late 18th and early 19th centuries; with European conflict again affecting colour supplies in the 1800s some glassmen resorted to lighter-toned substitutes such as amethyst. A deep purplish blue returned to favour in the 1820s, although today collectors revel especially in the rarer sets of decanters and glasses in shades of watery copper-green that became extremely dark, in thin glass, around 1800. This too was made at many glass centres— Bristol, Warrington, Edinburgh and elsewhere.

Ruby red at its best was a costly colour derived from gold chloride: hence the high value placed on Victorian cased or layered glass described in Chapter Eleven, which required a considerable thickness of the coloured glass fused over white and/or clear glass for deeply cut decanters and the like. A copper-derived ruby glass was developed in the 1820s. For some collectors the English term cranberry, later adopted in America, distinguishes this intense clear cherry colour from the Continent's harsher scarlet and later rosy pink. To others, cranberry is glass cheaply flashed with the ruby colour (effective as a background to wheel engraving). Flashing meant that the tinted molten glass was merely skimmed over clear glass before it was reheated and blown into shape. Stained glass in this connection is the term for colour brush-applied and fixed in a muffle kiln after the vessel has been shaped, so that pressed and moulded glass could be coloured and patterns introduced with stencils.

Yellow, often produced from chromate of lead, was popular late in the 19th century and a somewhat sickly greenish lemon yellow was all that most Victorians expected of uranium. This was described as 'opaline greenish colour' in the *Report of the Jury* of the Great Exhibition, 1851. The Report also listed a variety of colours such as violet from manganese, yellow from antimony, green from chromium, ruby or greenish-blue from copper, depending on the atmosphere created in the furnace. It was this welcome and increasing sophistication in the chemistry of glass that enabled the production of much of the art glass associated with the 1900s.

Silver was applied to glass by quite different techniques, most notably under an 1849 patent. In this the glass was blown double and the space between the two layers was filled with a silver solution through a hole in the bottom which was then sealed.

Equally interesting perhaps to those concerned with the glass-makers' crafts is the glass opacified to resemble white porcelain. 'Milk white glass and strong' had been ordered from Venice by John Greene, but it became more popular in the 1750s when English porcelain was itself a novelty and both wares could be decorated in all manner of fantasies with enamel colours and gold or, a little later, with transfer prints.

To Georgians this was enamel glass, as distinct from the high quality clear glass then called white flint and the nearly transparent cheap glass made from glasshouse waste and known as white glass. For example, in 1769 *The Newcastle Journal* advertised the New Glass House, Sunderland as selling 'flint-glass, white, enamel, blue and green'. Enamel glass found little favour with wine connoisseurs, but reduced versions of current decanter styles were made for table use, holding oil and vinegar and various sauces, sometimes labelled. The Bowles factory in Southwark was praised for its enamel glass as early as 1743 and in 1752 Dublin's Round Glasshouse offered 'mock china'. Bristol is often credited somewhat doubtfully with enamel glass of a particularly dense creamy whiteness assumed to have been made by opacifying a heavily leaded potash glass with the costly tin oxide familiar to the city's delftware potters who could also be called upon for decoration in the porcelain manner. In 1777, however, flint-glass became more heavily taxed and this enamel glass was included, encouraging manufacture of long familiar but inferior products, consisting of cheaply taxed soda-glass opacified to a milky white with either bone ash or arsenic. This milk glass was known also as sunset glow for its ruddy opalescence visible against the light. Many glasshouses made this ware in as many qualities, producing, for example, early-19th-century tankards and keepsake mugs painted and gilded or transfer-printed. Victorians could choose among many variants: R. Wilkinson in *The Hallmarks of Antique Glass* notes that 'the Richardson factory alone made over 100 mixtures of white glass and shipped plain articles all over Europe for factories to decorate.'

CHAPTER FIVE

Ornament

ANCIENT SYRIANS and Egyptians relished the beauty of vessels shaped by blowing air into their heated glass, and many other techniques still valued today were known in Roman days. However, the extraordinary variety of pattern and texture that delights the collector of English table glass was mainly developed here after George Ravenscroft evolved flint-glass: lustrous, gleaming and sturdy enough to take a wide range of ornament.

How best to bring out the light-dispersing beauty of this glass has been argued ever since, some welcoming its unique icicle sparkle and flashing fire revealed by deep cutting, others seeking fluent outlines to emphasise its limpid watery clarity. Increasingly severe taxes on glass from 1745 encouraged glassmen to make their decanters and drinking glasses light in weight with emphasis on decoration.

In the previous chapter I have referred to the patterning of glass in the course of shaping it by mould-blowing and pressing. Once aware of these alternatives the collector may seek out the various forms of cutting and wheel-engraving that figure most importantly in the decoration of free-blown glassware.

Engraving with the hard point of a diamond—practised on a small scale from early days—is rare on English table glass, but was popular with Dutch and Flemish glassmen, including stipple engraving from the 17th century with the diamond lightly tapped over the glass. Collectors of glass decorated in the Low Countries differentiate between the diamond-point stipple engraving of Frans Greenwood and David Wolff, for example, and the wheel-engraving of Jacob Sang. But usually here in Britain the decoration has been achieved by wheel engraving, which, like cutting, came to Britain from Germany and Bohemia. Engravers and cutters use a range of revolving wheels or discs to grind patterns into the glass, the only really major improvement down the centuries coming when steam power early in the 19th century—and still later

33. (*Left*) Fascinating engraving of a drinking party, the men holding their glasses by the foot in the manner of the day. Arms of 'Willaim of Wickham' on the reverse. Knopped air twist stem; *c.* 1750.

34. (*Right*) Decanter cut all over with shallow diamonds and fluting in the style that preceded heavy diamond cutting.

electricity–took over from the erratic movement of the early wheel-boy or the cutter's foot treadle, facilitating a wider range of decoration.

For cutting formal geometrical patterns the wheels could be comparatively large, but the fine decorative and pictorial ornament of wheel engraving required many smaller discs, traditionally of copper fed with oil and emery. It is not always realised that even the most elaborate patterns of flowers and rococo flourishes worked into the glass surface of mid-18th-century cordial glasses, for example, were produced by tiny strokes from a range of small wheels.

Early Georgian wheel-engravers largely developed their craft on the lighter style of glassware that then suited the period's tastes, made available by technical improvements in the glass itself widely known by the 1740s and doubtless encouraged by the new

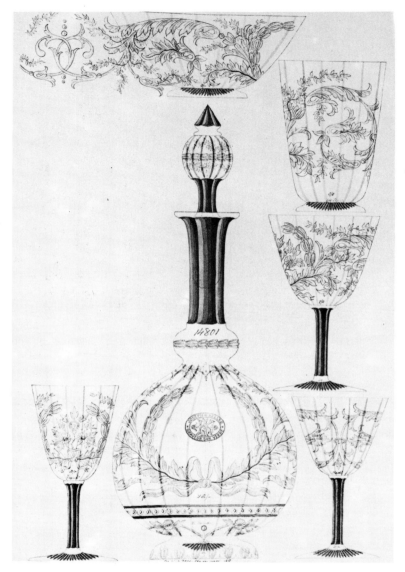

35. Design no. 214 from a volume entitled *A Collection of Patterns for the Use of Glass Decorators* by Joseph Keller, *c.* 1870.

36. Spirit decanter (right) with gold ruby casing, diamond cutting and lapidary stopper. Mallet shaped spirit bottle (left) blue cased, with an intaglio floral pattern. Royal Brierley Crystal, Brierley Hill.

glass tax calculated on weight. As described by R. Wilkinson, the artist-engraver, resting his elbows on padded rings on his work-bench, offered up the glass vessel to the revolving wheel from be-low. Inevitably this wonderfully skilled freehand work reveals uneven depths and jagged edges when examined under a magnify-ing glass.

Occasionally such engraving is armorial: Benjamin Payne of London advertised in about 1735 'the arms of all the Royal Family finely engraved on glasses'. Collectors note the change from early plain shields to the mid-18th-century curves among increasingly ornate flourishes of scrollwork. This was followed in the 1770s by Adam-style floral festoons, the shield itself spade-shaped with a scalloped top, until this in turn yielded to the plain forms of the 1800s.

Some engraving in the neo-classical style of the 1760s to 1780s is

37. Two claret decanters and a glass with engraved, etched and diamond-point
sgraffito ornament, 1900. Royal Brierley Crystal, Brierley Hill.

particularly attractive, including swags, urns, paterae, husks and
the like. Other work is commemorative (*see* Chapter Thirteen),
but often the ornament is basically decorative. Sometimes it is
even useful, as in the so-called label decanter, advertised as being
'new fashioned' in 1755, or the familiar drinking glass for strong ale
engraved with hop trails and ears of barley. In Chapter Three I
have described some of the motifs wheel-engraved on drinking
glasses to indicate their purpose. More wheel-engraving on rummers and the like might indicate ownership by an individual or
tavern or propose a toast to the success of a society or enterprise.

Some of this work is masterly, such as many ships in full sail, but
through the 18th and early 19th centuries pictorial engraving as
fine as brushwork was developed with especial delicacy by Bohemian and Silesian craftsmen on their hard unleaded glass, becoming
familiar in England through the imports permitted by the *Treaty of
Utrecht*, 1713. A number of these Continental craftsmen settled in

the West Midlands; during the second half of the 19th century surface engraving was elaborated, becoming, in effect, low relief carving in cameo and intaglio. The Victorian pleasure in such techniques applied to table glass that had been cased or flashed with colour, and in the limpid watery beauty of polished 'rock crystal' engraving, is referred to in Chapter Eleven.

In Victorian days hydrofluoric acid might be used instead of wheel-engraving, the design being scratched through a resist to allow the acid to etch the glass. The effect could suggest the clear detail of a photograph, but was used too for minor conventional ornament. A few 19th-century rummers have been found with the word PATENT on the base, the ornament sometimes being mistaken for etching: these according to Hugh Wakefield may have come from John Davenport who took out a patent in 1806. His process consisted of drawing a pattern in a covering of powdered glass paste on the glass surface which was then fixed by firing.

From c. 1870 the other alternative, sand blasting, also required the glass surface to be protected by a resist or stencil plate. It was then bombarded by a stream of sand or other abrasive of the required fineness; on drinking vessels such work was largely restricted to such details as weights-and-measures marks.

During the 18th century, as glassmen gradually gained greater control over the quality of their metal and the annealing that strengthened their vessels, glass-cutters, as distinct from glass wheel-engravers, became increasingly adventurous. They first ground out their pattern with comparatively large wheels of water-cooled sandstone or of iron fed with water and a sand abrasive, perhaps followed by finer emery (still later carborundum). Wooden discs then polished the pattern, fed with pumice, rotten stone and putty powder (calcined tin), perhaps followed by felt or cork fed with rouge (colcothar). More recently it was found that a brilliant gloss could be secured with a mixture of hydrofluoric and sulphuric acid.

Many collectors consider that cutting was at its finest in the 1770s to 1790s. Decanters and drinking glasses then were lightly cut in scoops and slicings to make very shallow diamond and hexagonal facets, never more exquisite than in facet-cut drinking glass stems.

Eventually, from early in the 19th century, glass-cutters created formal patterns by grinding deep into thicker glass with their rounded, v-shaped and flat panel wheel-cuts to suggest the sparkle of massive diamond jewellery. This may confuse those new to the techniques of glass decoration for this deep wheel cutting (and not the work with a diamond point) is what is almost always implied by the term diamond cutting. Steam power was in use at Stourbridge by 1807: the cutter still required much skill, but could ensure greater uniformity for patterns cut with a greater range of wheels.

The heavy tax on glass-by-weight meant that deeply cut (and therefore thick) glass was a considerable luxury – becoming part of the late Georgian's proud declaration of wealth and status. However, some of course was supplied from Ireland under a free trade agreement from 1780, many Englishmen working there until Irish glass, too, was taxed (Chapter Fourteen).

By grinding away intersecting v-shaped hollows (mitre cutting) the cutter could produce areas covered with sharply pointed diamonds known as relief diamonds and, when smaller, as fields of fine diamonds. If the cuts were more widely spaced, he produced larger, flat-topped diamonds and these could be further cut: in the most obvious cross-cut pattern; or, into groups of sixteen fine diamonds (strawberry pattern); or, more elaborately into groups of four star shapes (hobnail cutting). Straight v-cuts were known as splits and when forming a series of vertical or horizontal ridges the decoration was known as prismatic cutting often, less exactly, called step cutting. Brick-like arrangements of short prism cuts (alternate prisms) were particularly difficult to execute.

Bands of massed diamond points might be intersected by broad flat-bottomed panel cuts and edged with flutes or ridges in fan outlines or in the zig-zag outlines known as blazes. Other named patterns included rounded hollows known as printies. The wealth-declaring glitter achieved by Regency days may appear overdone today, but should be seen in a setting of candlelight among, say, Worcester's brilliant japan-patterned porcelain dinner wares – remembering always that English and Irish flint-glass, rich in lead, responded incomparably well to deep cutting because of its unique powers of refraction and reflection.

Through Victorian days competition from cheap pressed glass

38. Left to right. Sapphire blue tumbler with engraved cypher. Pomona green
tall hock glass. Wine glass in 'Cairngorm' amber with multiple ring stem.
Wine glass in 'tapestry' effect with the bowl entirely glass threaded and then
delicately enamelled with a floral design, *c.* 1880. Royal Brierley Crystal,
Brierley Hill.

prompted increasingly rich deeply cut arrangements of the
stereotyped geometrical motifs until the whole surface of a decanter or claret jug might be broken up into an extravaganza of
prismatic points. This won envious admiration even from the
Bohemians, but prompted indignation in the 1860s to 1870s
among the purists including John Ruskin.

An attractive detail sometimes found as a centrepiece to deep
cutting was the late Georgian *cristallo ceramie* or cameo incrustation,
originally a French notion patented in 1819 and copied less perfectly by mid-Victorians. Demonstrating how layers of hot glass
could fuse together imperceptibly, the younger Apsley Pellatt of
London's Falcon Glasshouse decorated table ware with small bas
relief celebrity portraits and the like, called sulphides. These were
mould-cast separately in a silvery china clay mixture which, as he

described in *Curiosities of Glassmaking*, 1849, had to 'harmonise with the density of the glass'. With great care taken to avoid unwanted air bubbles, they were wholly enclosed within clear glass such as the side of a decanter and its stopper finial, further patterned by deep cutting.

Many subjects were taken from medals and coins, such as George III, Queen Charlotte, Princess Charlotte, Wellington, Napoleon. Very occasionally one is found marked on the back 'Pellatt & Green' or 'Pellatt & Co'.

The most obvious form of decoration for the light-weight, thin-walled table glass popular around the mid-18th century, however, was surface colour and gilding, long applied to the less lustrous Continental glass. For this ornament the glass decorators could use techniques then beginning to be applied to porcelain and the bijouteries known as painted enamels. Enamel colours (powdered glass coloured with metallic oxides) were mixed with suitable fluxes to reduce their melting point and with an easily burnt-away vegetable oil so that they could be brush-painted onto the glass. In an enamelling (or muffle) kiln carefully applied heat ensured that the colour was fused on to the surface of the vessel without damaging its shape. This has proved more lasting than ornament in oil colours merely hardened onto the glass with a dessicator.

Most famous enameller on glass was William Beilby, 1740–1819, who with his sister Mary, 1749–97, came to Newcastle in 1760, their working period assumed to be from *c.* 1762 to 1778 when William left to teach drawing in London. They may have been assisted by their brother Ralph, a silversmith specialising in heraldic engraving, but even a rare signed Beilby piece seldom gives more than the surname. An exception in the Fitzwilliam Museum, Cambridge is a goblet signed *W. Beilby jun* *N Castle inv* *& pinx*. William had been apprenticed to a Birmingham decorator of painted enamels and no doubt the range of their work was enriched by long association with the delightful wood engraver Thomas Bewick, Ralph's apprentice and later partner. Another brother, Thomas, like William, taught drawing and enamelling.

Items presumed to bear Beilby enamel ornament include mallet-shaped decanters, goblets and wine glasses decorated in full colour or more usually in a bluish-white enamel to harmonise with their

39, 40. Two views of a tumbler splendidly enamelled in full colour with the royal arms of George III and probably commemorating the birth of the Prince of Wales in 1762; height 4¾ ins. Victoria and Albert Museum, London.

characteristic white-twist stems. Among armorial work a very few notable goblets with large bucket bowls bear George III's arms in full colour and the Prince of Wales's Feathers, probably commemorating the birth of George Augustus Frederick in 1762. Armorials might also be made up in the Continental manner, some introducing touches of colour such as turquoise. The Beilbys are credited, too, with Masonic and other commissioned work in addition to more fanciful subjects—perhaps by Mary Beilby— including fruiting vines, birds, flowers, all with a welath of delicate detail, picturesque landscapes in the ruin-and-obelisk style of their day, and pastimes such as skating, doubtless inspired by Bewick's work. In technique too the delicate linework suggests the engraver.

Ornament thought to be by the Beilbys may be found on drinking glasses that have stem-and-foot characteristics associated with the Tyneside area (Chapter Eight) and come from the old-established glasshouse of Dagnia-Williams. However, it appears likely from the quality of some of the enamel that not all of it was the work of the Beilbys, and obviously the style could be faked: despite long tradition even the inclusion of a butterfly, then a common enough motif, is not proof of a genuine piece. It is important to mention too that beginner-collectors should always be aware of imported white-painted 'Mary Gregory' glass (Chapter Eleven).

Beilby glasses are frequently rimmed in gold but this has worn badly and it must be assumed that it was not 'fired on'. The particularly attractive effects of even the simplest gold ornament on glass are associated with another name, Birmingham-born Michael Edkins, 1733–1811, who used both enamels and gold. He decorated glass for several Bristol firms from the early 1760s at a time when many other decorators were at similar work on glass and porcelain and South Staffordshire painted enamels. Edkins' ledgers record painting on opaque white enamel glass and 'cans' and beakers in blue glass. Interestingly Lazarus Jacobs of Bristol, d. 1796, and his son Isaac, gilder to George III, mentioned in Chapter Four, employed Edkins from 1785 to 1787 and he may well have been responsible for some of the sets of blue and green glass decanters 'labelled' in gold. A set of spirit decanters in Bristol City Art Gallery in a rich purplish blue are labelled in gold and signed in script *I. Iacobs Bristol*.

Gilding could be fixed like enamels by heat in a decorator's muffle kiln but all too often even on sets of decanters and cases of spirit squares—less freely handled than drinking glasses—mere traces of it remain, having been attached inadequately with an oil adhesive. But some delightful gold ornament of the 1760s to 1770s, kiln fixed, on opaque white and coloured glass is attributed to decorators in the London Soho workshops of the 'chinaman and enameller' James Giles, 1718 to 1780. This includes exotic birds among a wealth of feathery foliage and entwining vines. A Christie sale catalogue of his workshops' wares listed opaque white glass beakers with gilt decoration, pairs of decanters, cruet sets, sweetmeat, syllabub and jelly glasses and lemonade cups.

So much of this work is entirely anonymous that collectors note with some interest even the simple souvenir inscriptions, in gilt or enamel, on glass mugs, goblets and tumblers which are associated with William Absolon of Yarmouth who was active *c.* 1790 to 1810. These might be signed underneath.

Simpler ornament was sometimes introduced by making patterns out of the glass itself. Among the more obvious are the small raised bosses known as prunts (the opposite of the hollowed-out printies mentioned earlier). These were applied to the stems of some mas-

41. Victorian skills shown in drinking glass ornament. Left: very slender
version of the twist stem; enamelling on the bowl. Left-centre: engraved,
c. 1880. Right-centre and right: late-19th-century Richardson glass –
ruby-stained and frosted, and cut and enamelled work on cased glass.
Broadfield House Glass Museum, Kingswinford.

sive goblets in the late 17th and early 19th centuries, often surface-
tooled and then called raspberry or strawberry prunts and I refer
to them again among Victorian novelties. But the most challenging
work consisted of thin trails of glass built up as series of loops
around the rims of some 18th-century stemmed glasses intended
not for liquor but for dessert sweetmeats. Victorians wound finer
threads of glass round some rims, stems and handles.

Still more obvious decoration consisted merely of air bubbles.
Dents were made in the hot glass and covered with more glass so
that the trapped air swelled into bubble shapes. An early drinking
glass might contain merely a single bubble below the bowl,
elongated into a drop and known as a tear. But it was found that
when glass containing a group of air beads was drawn out and

42. (*Left*) Finely gilded goblet with gilded rim and cusped facet-cut stem, the decoration ascribed to the workshops of James Giles.

43. (*Right*) Goblet ascribed to William Beilby, *c*. 1770. The arms are those of Richard Loundes, Buckinghamshire, enamelled in red, azure and gold. Opaque white twist stem; height 8½ ins. Corning Museum of Glass, New York.

twisted and then covered with more glass the result could be a smooth-surfaced stem filled with spiralling silvery threads, described by W. B. Honey as 'among the chief English inventions in glass of the mid 18th century'.

The idea probably developed when glassmen in the late 1730s began experimenting with improvements on still earlier wrythen bowls and knops. They found they could incise a stem with vertical ribs and then immediately twist the hot glass, achieving the effect of a shallow incision spiralling down its length – an inconspicuous, but extremely pleasing, variant of the plain straight stem. An early stem may show a very slight narrowing towards the centre.

A drawn air-twist stem might even include a swelling knop, but it proved easier, of course, to make such stems separately as long rods of unvarying thickness that could be cut to the required length for a three-part glass. It even proved possible to vary the air-twists by combining, say, the most usual multiple spiral of narrow corkscrew ribbons with a central core of 'gauze' or a pair of spiralling corkscrew ribbons with a central closely twisted cable, making what collectors style a compound twist stem. A composite twist stem was built up by combining plain and twist stem sections, separated perhaps by a beaded knop—not always with happy results but produced with very great skill.

Some of the most brilliantly clear glass stems with wide reflective air spirals are mistakenly called mercury twists, but often of course enamels were used for the twists in such stems in colours, mainly blue or green with red and in opaque white, again depending on the marvellous capacity of hot glass to fuse and to be drawn out without distortion. In colour twists the style of such gaily stemmed glasses agreed perfectly with the lighthearted rococo delicacy seen in contemporaneous porcelains.

The opaque white and colours were introduced as canes or rods of costly enamel around the inside of a cylindrical metal mould. This was then filled with clear glass and the resultant vertically striped rod was coated with more clear glass to form a short thick cylinder. A couple of men reheated and stretched and twisted this into a slender cane which could be cut to the required lengths for stems.

The millefiori (thousand flower) arrangements occasionally found in decanter-stopper finials show another application of this ancient Roman ornament by ingenious Victorians. Small cylinders of glass were built up with concentric layers of colour and elong-ated into slender canes. Slices cut from differently patterned canes were arranged on a bed of clear glass with more glass fused over them in a low dome that appeared to be filled with their colours.

CHAPTER SIX

Earliest Decanters and Glasses

1680s to 1730s

THE PERIOD that evolved flint-glass table wares also witnessed a new sophistication in wine decanting. It was customary then to bring wines to table in substantial dark blackish-green or brown bottles in coarse workaday glass, praised by R. J. Charleston as 'an English speciality envied by Continental Europe'. The typical 17th-century bottle with its long tapering neck and nearly spherical body (a design traditional in Roman and Venetian glass too) is known to collectors as the shaft-and-globe. It has a narrow 'string ring' below the mouth for securing the sealed cork and the characteristic base is pushed inwards in a dome or 'kick'. A glass seal might be applied in the course of making the bottle so as to identify its owner, for the wealthy usually bought their wine by the cask from the vintner and sent their own bottles to be filled and corked.

An interesting alternative vessel was a more costly lightweight flask with a rounded base – a flask was defined by Bailey in 1730 as a 'sort of bottle wrought over with wicker twigs' which protected the thin glass and gave it the name of wanded bottle. It was used especially for bottling champagne and for bringing it unopened to table in a silver or other ornamental container.

There is ample evidence that wine might have been matured in the bottle by binning as early as the 17th century, the sealed bottles laid slopewise in sand in a cellar to ensure that the cork did not dry out. However, if clear wine was to be offered at table it was essential to pour it gently into a suitable vessel without disturbing the sediment: this was decanting as defined in Kersey's dictionary in 1715.

Obviously for greatest effect the decanter had to be of clear glass to reveal the quality of the wine; it is not surprising to find that some of the earliest flint-glass decanters made by Ravenscroft resembled the long necked round-bodied shaft-and-globe bottles. The actual decanting proved difficult – prompting the jug design, also made by Ravenscroft, with a neck widening into a cup shape (a Venetian pattern). This was soon outmoded when a funnel was

44. (*Left*) Late-17th-century decanter-jug, the substantial flint-glass blown into a mould to form the body ribs and strengthened with added glass ornament round the neck and shoulders. Victoria and Albert Museum, London.
45. (*Centre*) Decanter jug of the 1720s, octagonal on plan in the manner of contemporaneous silver, with a ball finial to the tapering stopper.
46. (*Right*) Modified versions of the cruciform or lobed decanter with stringing round their long necks, that on the left showing wrythen moulding.

used for filling from the bottle so as to avoid aerating the wine. Substantial flint-glass shaft-and-globe decanters in quart and pint sizes continued well into Georgian days. These must not be confused with Victorian examples which were heavily cut in the mid 19th century, becoming more popular later as light-weight vessels distinguishable by the quality of the glass.

From the few remaining 17th-century flint-glass decanters the collector notes such other early characteristics as the handles and beak spouts seen on some Ravenscroft vessels, making them comparable with wine jugs in delftware. Ravenscroft's price-list in 1677 indicated a range of decanter styles, some ornamented with prunts and trailed threads of glass, some with frilled neck and foot rings to associate them with long-cherished Venetian fashions: collectors often class the late 17th century as the Anglo-Venetian period.

Stoppers associated with the wide-necked vessels were high domes, hollow blown, with looped or knopped finials. (Doubtless many were made with crown finials at this time.) However, with such easily broken items, style dating is difficult. A vessel in the Museum of London still possesses its hollow stopper tapering at the bottom almost to a point to ensure an airtight fit. These appear to have been followed soon by solid-pinched stoppers as an alternative to the customary corks or parchment-covered wooden wedges.

This obvious advance is indicated by John Worlidge's instruction on stopper grinding in *Cider*, 1675:

> With a turn [lathe] made for that purpose you may grind glas stopples to each bottle . . . each stopple having a button on top . . . the mouths of your bottles are similarly ground.

This refinement is very seldom noted among the comparatively few decanters that remain from the early 18th century. The neck ring used to secure the pack thread fastening the cork to the bottle could prove even more useful, as Worlidge suggested, for a thread ensured that the stopper stayed with the bottle it was ground to fit. Round or knife-edged it became a decorative detail, for it checked dribbles and also helped the user to obtain a firm grip on the heavy vessel.

Englishmen quickly realised the real advantages of the sturdy new flint-glass and Venetian fancies were forgotten while heavy decanters in the plain outlines of the shaft-and-globe bottle continued well into the 18th century. With the early ring foot soon abandoned, the base of the globular body, as in common bottles, was pressed inward to form a high 'kick' which trapped hot air and was an aid to early annealing. By the 1730s better annealing permitted a less pronounced kick in the base but it still kept the pontil scar from scratching the dining table.

Meanwhile, in the 1700s decanters were developing more interesting outlines, with the neck still as long as the body or slightly longer but with more or less square shoulders and straight or very slightly inward-tapering sides, some circular, others hexagonal or octagonal on plan, harmonising with early Georgian silver. The shape suggested a sculptor's mallet and they are therefore usually known as mallet decanters, although this term is used by some collectors for a later shape. They might be fitted with cone-shaped finials and date mainly to *c.* 1710 to 1740. Both shaft-and-globe and mallet decanters are found occasionally with strap handles.

With the body tooled into four deep lobes the quatrefoil or cruciform decanter, *c.* 1720s to 1750s, was designed to allow quick cooling of the liquor when the vessel was immersed in an icy wine cistern. A trade card in the British Museum illustrates one used for cider. These are now rare, but there is a good example in the Cecil Higgins Museum, Bedford.

The earliest style of drinking glass required in English flint-glass is indicated by the hundreds of illustrations that were sent by John Greene to his Venetian agent Morelli, *c.* 1670, the English glasses of the 1680s to 1690s also being classified by collectors as Anglo-Venetian. But these large, substantial vessels took on more assured, finely proportioned English styles around the turn of the century, enriched rather than dominated by the various Continental notions that came in with the courts of Dutch William III and Hanoverian George I and by the flood of imports that followed the *Treaty of Utrecht* in 1713. An exception has already been referred to in Chapter Three: the roemer goblet with almost spherical bowl, narrowing slightly to the rim, on a hollow prunt-decorated stem, a copy of German–Dutch imports. A broader shallower cup bowl may be noted, too, with gadrooning around the base; this is now often described as a mead glass.

Always any consideration of drinking glasses implies assessment of bowl and stem and foot, the different shapes and patterns having been given more or less obvious and widely accepted names. Late-17th-century bowls were most usually deep, straight-sided funnels or still narrower flutes, thick towards the base and often decorated with moulding or – like some very early decanters – with added glass pincered into ribs or the 'smocking' described at the time by Ravenscroft as 'nip't diamond waies'. Sometimes the added moulding that surrounded the bowl was twisted into whirls ('wrythen') or pincered into flammiform, or flame-shaped, frills, again excellent for masking murky ale or any sediment in the wine. (Soon the wrythen ornament was worked into the single thickness of the glass bowl.) But it was the stem style that changed most conspicuously during the 18th century and for those of the first period, say 1680 to 1730, the collector term is baluster, taken from the simplest vase or urn outline as used by architect and silversmith.

Stems in the 1680s to 1690s were still short, although Greene designs reflected the importance already attached to small differences in pattern. There is evidence that some Anglo-Venetian flint-glass glasses had hollow baluster stems. But most interesting, perhaps, was the way in which such hollow-blown stems found an echo in the air bubbles or comma-shaped tears sometimes introduced into the plain solid little balls and balusters that more usually linked the deep early bowls to the wide feet of 17th-century English glasses. A point to note on drinking glasses of this period and on through the 18th century is that the bowl rim was frequently a slightly smaller circle than the foot.

In the late 17th century the usual foot shape was a low cone which served to raise the rough pontil scar beneath it well clear of the table top. But the most conspicuous detail was the foot's folded rim. This had been important in strengthening Venetian soda-glass. In flint-glass the rim was folded narrowly under the foot at first but often a little more widely in the early 18th century. Upward folded feet may be noted on some Continental glass. In articles as pleasantly individualistic as drinking glasses it is impossible to be too specific and many glasses are found with bowl rim and foot of equal width. Folded feet seldom chip but always a plain foot may have been ground down at the edge later to remove such a blemish.

So much for the brief Anglo-Venetian years. Even before 1700, as glassmen throughout the country developed their skill at blowing flint-glass table wares, a wider range of shapes became established. By c. 1710 an occasional alternative to the simple conical or funnel bowl was a funnel with a rounded base, the outline sometimes becoming more nearly square in the bucket bowl, suitable for a large goblet, in contrast to the waisted bell shape that soon became very popular. Characteristically the bowl ended in a deep solid base and this, in a funnel or bell bowl, might contain a tear; occasionally it was rounded so that the bowl outline attractively suggested a thistle. However, from the end of the 17th century onwards bowls yielded in decorative importance to an extraordinary complexity of stem design, fascinating to those experts who must try to date every shape within a decade.

Clearly one outline led to another, but probably for most of us it is most helpful to compare drinking-glass stems with similar combinations of ball and vase, cushion and spool and 'Portuguese swell' among the outlines of contemporary stemmed silver ware and the turned legs of newly fashionable chairs and side tables.

Tall flute bowls on rudimentary stems continued too, of course; in contrast the 'tall ale' goblet might have a stem even longer than its characteristic deep bowl, while in smaller-bowled glasses for wines and spirits the difference became even more marked.

From *c.* 1700 an occasional splendid glass remains with a deep bowl on a stem of 'pure' baluster form—or more often in the shouldered shape of the inverted baluster. At its simplest this was drawn smoothly down from the bowl in a two-piece or straw-shank vessel, the dusky glass lightened in the swelling by a large tear.

For many other drinking glasses of the 1700s to 1730s, however, the collector's most generally accepted stem terminology is not very helpful: heavy balusters until *c.* 1710 or 1715; light balusters, *c.* 1710 to 1735, and balustroids from *c.* 1725 to 1760. Hence the importance of the term knop for the knobs and swellings that enriched the stems' outlines throughout this chapter's period.

Knops too have their descriptive names including the shoulder knop or cushion which, when still further compressed, may be called an angular or bladed knop; the annulated knop composed of three, five or even seven contiguous rings; the attractive acorn or mushroom knop; the spreading drop knop; the straight-sided clumsy looking cylinder knop and inward-sloping cone knop and the rare swelling egg-shape knop. Often enough the collector faced with an elaborate composition of such shapes prefers to settle for the term multi-knop stem.

Glasses in the early heavy baluster category are typically sturdy vessels ranging from spirit glasses, perhaps less than five inches tall, through wine glasses, often six or seven inches, to goblets and ale flutes, sometimes nine inches or more. A typical thick stem might be composed of a finger-inviting inverted baluster or a mushroom or acorn knop often wider than the bowl's heavy rounded base and supported on a smaller ball knop above the wide, high-stepping folded foot; sometimes two inverted balusters, head to head, formed the stem. The large air bubble filling the main baluster or knop was often extended into an elongated tear from *c.* 1720.

The Kit-Cat glass must be mentioned here, a vessel with a heavy-based plain funnel bowl on a tall knop-and-baluster stem and folded foot. Such a glass is to be seen in the portrait of the Duke of

47. (*Far left*) Magnificent early glass showing the typical deep rounded-funnel bowl with a thick base above the substantial stem, its knop containing a well-shaped tear; the foot folded.

48. (*Left*) Support for Queen Anne (1702–14) on a heavy glass with a fine acron knop in the stem and a wide folded foot.

49. (*Right*) An interesting glass, its bell bowl engraved with an orange tree (for the House of Orange) and the inscription *For Ever Flourishing*. The stem shows the transition from knopped to straight outlines. Wide domed and folded foot. George II's reign. Brooklyn Museum, New York.

50. (*Far right*) The white horse of Hanover and inscription *Aurea Libertas* on an English glass with a fine moulded pedestal stem, *c.* 1745–50.

Newcastle by Sir Godfrey Kneller, now in the National Portrait Gallery among a series painted 1703 to 1720 showing members of the Whig Club that met at a pie-house run by Christopher (Kit) Catling. The Duke holds his glass by the foot in the manner fashionable *c.* 1660 to 1760 while filling it from a wanded wine flask such as I mention at the beginning of this chapter.

By *c.* 1715 the great demand for everyday drinking glasses prompted lighter, less grandiose versions of the heavy baluster glass. In these 'light balusters' the stems still retained much of the early shapeliness but in more slender outlines, the baluster or inverted baluster no longer broader than any accompanying knops. This stem was particularly well suited to the popular bell and thistle bowls. But by at least as early as the 1720s many stems had lost the baluster motif, being composed instead of a series of knops shaped, it might seem, according to the gaffer's whim as he or his servitor gyrated and tooled the stem's hot glass at the chair, not always with much apparent sense of form and proportion and often enough in the wake of fashion, using glass of poor quality (tale metal from the top or bottom of the melting pot).

These collector-termed balustroid glasses also tended to become more slender and lighter in weight during this period. Towards the mid-century fashion found delightful new shapes and ornament for drinking glasses, but balustroids continued well into the second half of the century, especially in so-called Newcastle glasses. But more about these in Chapter Eight.

A quite different style of stem appeared as a much briefer fashion on early-18th-century drinking vessels (although continuing on sweetmeat glasses into the 1750s to 1760s). This was the moulded pedestal stem (strictly an inverted pedestal with a downward taper). It was a Continental shape that may have preceded George I's arrival from Hanover in 1714, which is the curious reason often suggested for its popular name of silesian stem. Its moulded shaping suggests a bolder, more angular and deeply fluted treatment of the inverted baluster – perhaps too heavy for its bowl.

It might be four-sided at first with a rounded funnel bowl and occasionally the flat surfaces of the stem proved tempting for a toast or political slogan. However, the moulded pedestal is more often found as a six- or eight-sided pillar. In its later versions the stem was often linked to a double-ogee bowl and a domed foot by knops or collars variously decorated with air beads or spiral tooling.

While these were the main styles of drinking glass sought by collectors to represent this important and very splendid period, it must be remembered that the still earlier tall flute bowls on rudimentary stems continued too, many apparently intended for rough tavern use.

The early conical folded foot described above continued beyond the end of this period. Indeed, the beginner-collector must remember that folded feet in the early style were still acceptable on cheap wine glasses and spirit drams as late as the 1830s. But long-fashionable variants introduced on baluster glasses included: the foot with a central dome surrounded by a broad, nearly flat rim; the terraced foot rising to a central dome in a series of ridges; and the foot shaped with a circle of radiating ribs.

CHAPTER SEVEN

Early Georgian Decanters

1730s to 1780s

How PAMPERED with pleasures were well-to-do early Georgians, their elegant homes sparkling with sophisticated new furnishings in the light-hearted style now called rococo. Around the mid-18th century furniture and ornaments might be decorated with complexities of asymmetrical patterns such as opposing c-scrolls, often introducing frivolous neo-Gothic architectural detail and even more beguiling Chinamen and other chinoiseries carved, gilded or coloured in vivid japanning. Earthen table wares were being challenged by delicate porcelains – some English-made from the later 1740s – and glassmen had sufficient mastery over the shaping and annealing of their wares to manufacture decanters and drinking glasses of a lightness and decorative charm to match their surroundings.

Admittedly, all the shapes familiar in England's 18th-century table glass may be found too in Continental glass, sometimes described as *façon d'Angleterre*. But these lacked, of course, the rich lustrous brilliance of English flint-glass and often were less carefully finished in such details as the smoothing of pontil scars.

The *Excise Act* of 1745 began modestly enough, charging 9s. 4d. per hundredweight of the raw material; as a result the price of undecorated flint-glass rose by a penny per pound. This too must have been a factor encouraging manufacture of less massive decanters with a wholly new emphasis on ornament to justify their price.

The shaft-and-globe bottle style and the square-shouldered mallet of George I's day were unimaginative decanter shapes, albeit long retained. The new, more slender style favoured from *c*. the 1740s is known to the collector by the name of shouldered decanter: in this the neck was not so long in proportion to the body and the angle between neck and body less abrupt. Below the shoulder the body slanted a little towards the base, either inward on the broad-shouldered vessel or outward on the narrow-

51. (*Left*) Narrow-shouldered decanter engraved with fruiting vine and with its naming for Greek wine engraved to suggest a label or decanter ticket hung around its neck in the silversmith's manner. Lunar slicing on the inverted pear-shape stopper finial. Corning Museum of Glass, New York.

52. (*Centre*) Shaft-and-globe decanter shaped with 'Norwich' or 'Lynn' horizontal ribbing. Air tears in the round stopper finial; *c.* 1755.

53. (*Right*) Broad-shouldered decanter cut all over with shallow diamond-shaped facets which are reflected and multiplied into a rich pattern owing to the quality of the flint-glass, 1770s. Corning Museum of Glass, New York.

shouldered, bell-shaped variant. Better methods of annealing obviated the need for a high kick in the base which was shaped with no more than a slight dome. Smoothing of the pontil scar under the base became a minor detail when the vessel was being decorated by a glass-cutter. There was no longer a string ring at the neck and instead of a silver-mounted cork the stopper might be of glass with a solid ball or tall cone finial.

Despite the instructions of John Worlidge quoted in the previous chapter it appears that stopper and decanter mouth were seldom well ground to make an airtight fit until nearly the mid-century—an expected nicety by *c.* 1760. If a decanter is found with roughening only of the neck *or* of the stopper the assumption must be that they do not really belong to each other. (Collectors can be certain that a stopper is a replacement if it shows engraved or cut ornament while the decanter itself is not similarly decorated.) Decanters of the period are rare and doubtless many were discarded when ill-fitting stoppers became immovable, glass-makers welcoming back the broken glass 'cullet' as a part of their mixture that remained untaxed until 1777.

An obvious improvement dating from this time was the tapering stopper, no longer a straight cylinder, that fitted into a similarly tapered decanter mouth. Illustrations of the 1740s and later may show cylindrical, flat-topped stopper finials, but the more usual shape in the 1750s was the spire. Thomas Betts' many mid-century advertisements of his King's Arms Glass Shop even included 'Betts' Gothic' finials. Spires were followed in the 1760s by finger-pleasing vertical discs: when the disc was shaped with a central depression the finial was called a target or bull's-eye.

Decoration is the main source of our pleasure in the vessels of this period, giving interest to the glass surface without seriously obscuring the contents or interrupting the vessel's well-proportioned outline. Simplest ornament consists of the wide horizontal ribs, or very slight rounded swellings, perhaps as many as nine, around the body of a broad-shouldered vessel: these were known as Norwich or Lynn rings. But the rococo spirit was most delightfully expressed in the scrolling flourishes including innumerable elaborations of that most decorative of plants, the fruiting vine, that were worked by wheel-engraver, enameller and even gilder over shoulder and body.

Often these formed a magnificent cartouche (like those that bordered many a glass-seller's tradecard) around the name of a wine on what the period came to know as a label decanter. These were advertised for example in the *Norwich Weekly Mercury* in 1755 as 'new fashioned, with enscriptions engraven on them, Port, Claret, Mountain, etc. etc., decorated with vine leaves, grapes, etc.'. An easy way of indicating the contents of a decanter or bottle in the 18th to 19th centuries was to hang a small silver label or bottle ticket on a chain around its neck. The mid-18th-century glass engraver or enameller produced a more elaborate version of such a label's rococo ornament, often based on fruiting vines so that grapes and curling tendrils enlivened the whole front of the decanter, with a lozenge in the centre lettered with the wine. Greek wine and ale are among the most frequently found today. The final touch was a representation of the silver chain, engraved or enamelled, around the decanter's neck.

For a few years these vessels might be listed as 'flower'd and lettered decanters', becoming 'label decanters' in the early 1760s. If stock names did not suffice a customer could have the name of his choice engraved for a shilling or so. I have referred in Chapter Three to such ornament in both wheel-engraving and enamelling, but perhaps it is wise to emphasise again that such desirable labels may be modern additions to old plain decanters.

Here it is enough to note how soon such delicate engraving felt the competition of wheel cutting. At first the wide flat diamond cutting barely ruffled the glass surface, but it soon took the form of lightly hollowed-out facets. Facet-cut decanters, fashionable from about the mid-1760s, were infinitely more delicate and graceful than the heavily cut vessels of Regency and post-Regency years. Some were cut all over, the facets spiralling around neck and body and over the final. They were always light, shallow light-catching concavities, mostly diamond-shaped, or long diamonds or hexagons, giving a wonderful brilliance to the wine.

Sometimes the neck was enriched with scale pattern and the body with a circuit of stars or printies above finger flutes around the base. However, the 1760s saw fashion welcome the restrained grace of Robert Adam's neo-classical ornament. This prompted a range of familiar conventional motifs such as husk and sprig among pendant swags. An advertisement in the *Norwich Weekly Mercury* in 1771 offered 'cut, plain, sprig'd and engraved decanters'.

Fashion silhouettes of the period prompted a further tapering of the narrow-shouldered decanter to no more than a smooth swelling from neck to base cut with shallow flutes and facets. From *c.* 1770 the mouth might turn outwards in a lip known as a brim and by perhaps 1780 the smooth neck might be rendered easier to hold by an added neck-ring. This is known to collectors as the taper decanter. Its customary disc finial was edged at first with shallow diamond facets, followed by scalloping or half-moon 'lunar facets' around the edge, the faces of the disc being slightly hollowed. Soon the whole stopper finial, still a flat vertical disc, became slimmer too, following the period's favourite inverted pear outline.

54. Pair of barrel decanters cut with vertical flutes to suggest staves and horizontal rings to represent hoops. Inverted pear-shape stopper finials with bevelled edges, *c.* 1780.

The 1771 newspaper advertisement quoted above referred also to 'carrosts', the water carafe then known also as a water craft that the collector distinguishes from a decanter by its out-turned mouth or brim left smooth inside and without a stopper. In the 18th century a carafe of water with two goblets would be placed between each two diners. The carafe with matching tumbler inverted over its mouth was a detail of the Victorian bedroom.

Another vessel of the period was the large, narrow-shouldered decanter with a pocket for ice as described in Chapter Three. These were priced by Thomas Betts in the 1750s in quart size at twelve shillings a pair. For warm claret, handled, spouted jugs appeared occasionally again from *c.* 1770, sometimes facet-cut to match a pair of decanters.

Even slender taper decanters tended to be made of thicker glass as the century advanced, allowing for slightly deeper facet-cutting to give the vessels an effect of great brilliance. The taper outline continued into the 19th century, but from the 1770s a particularly attractive variant was the now rare pear-shaped or Indian club decanter (a term, like mallet, differently applied by some collectors). This was soon broadened a little to become known as the barrel decanter, a particularly well-balanced outline, its body still slender but rounded and distinguished by having shoulder and base of equal diameter, as well as being lightly cut with narrow flutes representing a barrel's hoops and staves. 'Curious barrel-shaped decanters cut on an entirely new pattern' were advertised by Christopher Haedy in the *Bath Chronicle* in 1775. By *c.* 1780 the vessel might have a wide thick brim with a vertical edge. The barrel notion was too pertinent to be forgotten quickly and must be mentioned again later when it became more flamboyant, if somewhat squat.

Meanwhile in complete contrast to the slender Indian-club outline was a contemporary vessel, the ship's decanter, which became known as a Rodney during the general acclamation that greeted this admiral's victories over the Spanish and the French in 1780 and 1782. This vessel, usually quart-size, was mainly, but by no means exclusively, for officers' use at sea. Occasionally a specimen is found in the comparatively thin, undecorated glass of perhaps 1770, forerunner of the more familiar later Georgian vessel which has a more rounded base giving an attractive line to this essential concentration of weight.

A characteristic feature of the vessel was the way that the sides of the body slanted directly from below the long, massive neck to the exceptionally wide base, without shoulder shaping. The decanter without its stopper might be as broad as it was tall. This meant that all the weight was in the lower part of the vessel, ensuring great stability.

When heavy cutting became usual the base might be ridged with a star-cut pattern to grip the baize-topped cabin table. The stopper

55. Pair of ships decanters cut with wide flutes. With target stopper finials, angular neck rings and star-cut bases.

finial of the 1770s to 1780s was usually a plain target or bull's-eye. This vessel is often found with as many as four or five applied neck-rings below the brim, to be grasped the more easily since the distribution of the weight made it particularly difficult to tilt for pouring.

A gradual return to neck-rings is observed on other decanters too from c. the 1770s and this marked the beginning of a general change to sturdier vessels, less easily toppled over and reflecting the tough, hard-living stalwarts who spent long and raucous nights in their company. Two or three neck-rings below a wide lip or brim were introduced on a somewhat shorter neck above a broad-shouldered body tapering only slightly to the base.

This provided the required change to a new emphasis on horizontal lines, frequently further stressed by broad and narrow flute cutting, especially around the lower half of the body. Typically the stopper had a massive vertical target finial. This from the 1780s was known as the Prussian decanter and all its variants dominated the period considered in Chapter Nine. Indeed it has never gone away. R. Wilkinson declares that millions have been made from the

18th century to modern times 'in liqueur, spirit, wine, claret, magnum and even larger sizes'.

Squares, or decanters that are square on plan, often with canted corners, may date from as early as somewhat similar mallet decanters. For mid-Georgians their main purpose appears to have been to fit six or twelve closely together in handsome, velvet-lined wooden cases, of mahogany perhaps, or covered in waterproof shagreen or sharkskin so that spirits or cordials – or, in smaller sizes, medicines and toilet water – could be kept under lock and key. Clearly some were intended to fortify the traveller.

Such vessels were usually mould-blown with space-saving high shoulders and short necks, their finials either air-beaded balls or small vertical discs. Some show traces of fleeting gilded ornament especially on the finial and around the shoulder so as to make a fine show when the case was opened. As late as 1851 the Great Exhibition included handsome 'regency cabinets' containing sets of squares and glasses.

Squares are difficult to date earlier than the labelled spirit sets, often in richly coloured glass, that were in use through the late years of the 18th century and the heavily cut sets that followed for the Victorian tantalus frame.

CHAPTER EIGHT

Early Georgian Glasses

1730S to 1780S

DRINKING GLASSES were surely never lovelier than during the period covered by this chapter. Technical improvements gradually gave the glass itself an almost water-clear brilliance, but never a bland characterless purity. Already by the late 1730s fashion was looking for lighter, more decorative vessels in livelier outlines and this trend was given a boost by the imposition of the Excise duty in 1745 that became far more onerous in 1777.

As indicated in Chapter Three, drinking glasses through this period ranged from the normal run of vessels for wines, strong ale, champagne and the like to the small-bowled elegance of cordial glasses. Squat utility shapes of tumbler and dram contrasted with the more massive proportions of goblets including various sizes of short-stemmed rummer.

To begin with their bowls, these still included the widely popular trumpet, bell, cone or flute, bucket, rounded funnel and thistle; also the occasional cup and deeper ovoid that narrowed slightly towards the rim. But by the 1730s new shapes, perhaps for champagne, included the wide bowl with a somewhat everted rim and the so-called pan-top bowl in an outline suggesting a saucer above a cup which some collectors regard as solely a syllabub-sweetmeat glass.

When the upper part of such a bowl is cup-shaped with an out-curving rim and is large in proportion to the narrower funnel shape below the vessel is known as a double ogee rather than pan-shaped, the ogee being another term borrowed from architecture, signifying an elongated s-shape. In the simple ogee bowl the sides of the vessel are nearly vertical for perhaps two-thirds of its depth, then rounded in to slant down to the stem. Occasionally such a bowl is six-sided or eight-sided. The ogee shape assumes a more definite s-silhouette when the bowl is slightly waisted – the waisted ogee.

One unusual style of rounded funnel bowl shows wide shallow

56. High quality glasses with double-ogee bowls and pedestal stems on decorative domed feet, controversially described as champagne or sweetmeat glasses, *c.* 1730s. One with fruiting vine engraving.

horizontal ribbing so that the outline is a series of very slight swellings or corrugations typically in notably clear glass, giving it an attractive shimmering effect. I have referred in Chapter Seven to decanters with similar shaping, known as Norwich or Lynn rings. Norwich Castle Museum has a number of these fine quality glasses.

The main development of the period, however, was that wine glasses, like decanters, often passed to another group of specialists quite distinct from the craftsmen who made the glass, to be enriched with motifs beyond the range of any moulded, 'hammered' or lattice effects achieved in the course of shaping the hot glass. Most important, of course, from the late 1730s, was the work of the wheel-engravers, with motifs in white enamel and gilding as occasional alternatives described in Chapter Five. Collectors welcome fruiting vine, hop-and-barley, cider apples and many more personal motifs and names engraved or enamelled on every kind of drinking glass bowl throughout the rest of the century. (*See* Chapter 13.)

By the 1730s it had become usual for the stem to be considerably longer than the bowl. This was most conspicuous in the balustroids first mentioned in Chapter Six that form a link between the early elaborations of baluster swellings and the mid-century change of emphasis in stems from shape to decoration. The tall light balustroid glasses of the 1730s to 1760s have prompted considerable discussion. Their metal – frequently of a fine clear quality – sometimes appears so thinly blown that it has been suggested, mistakenly, that less lead was used in their composition. However, a general similarity in the complexities of lightly knopped, somewhat spindly stems may well point to a common area of origin. Occasional Dutch engraving on their bowls, by Greenwood, Wolff, Schouman and others, appears to corroborate the speculation that Newcastle was the source, the familiar stem style being continued for the sake of a flourishing export trade. So Newcastle balustroid is now their name.

Typically the vessel is a three-piece glass, perhaps seven or eight inches tall, the narrow-based trumpet or rounded funnel bowl supported on a stem composed of a number of different small motifs. These may include, for example, a beaded knop above a thin cylinder knop, above an inverted baluster, culminating in another beaded knop above a plain or domed foot that often lacks the protective folded edge.

By the 1730s to 1740s the moulded pedestal stems referred to in Chapter Six were usually eight-sided, but becoming less generally fashionable. However they continued into the 1760s as somewhat more slender supports for wide bowls – ogee, double-ogee and pan-shape – associated with dessert table sweetmeats such as syllabubs and (probably briefly) with champagne.

More surprising, perhaps, was the main stem development through the 1730s to the 1760s, and continuing thereafter, in plain straight outlines. Short lengths of straight stem (so-called cylinder knops) often filled much of a light balustroid 'Newcastle' stem. But here was a new interest in the straight silhouette, doubtless influenced by the wish to save weight and therefore tax after 1745. And just as engraving transformed a simple drinking-glass bowl, so clever ornamental detail was introduced into these otherwise

57. (*Left*) Light baluster stem in the manner ascribed to Newcastle, the coat of arms probably engraved in Holland; height 18·3 cm.

58. (*Right*) Pair of goblets with double-knop air twist stems, the bowls delicately engraved with butterflies and fruiting vine.

prosaic stems. Most obvious design was the two-piece glass with a trumpet bowl smoothly drawn into a slightly tapering or very slightly waisted stem no longer including the inverted baluster swelling that ensured easy grasping of the early heavy vessel.

Sometimes the drawn stem flows almost as smoothly into a plain conical foot, although often this difficult junction is given a more pleasing line with a small knop, and occasionally with domed-foot shaping. This was a cheap glass for early Georgian home and tavern made in great numbers and many sizes down to drams. On the three-piece (stuck-shank) glass the line of junction between bowl and stem is often uncompromisingly plain, even with a wide-based bucket bowl, but late in the century a strengthening merese or knop might be introduced. In these stems, too, the collector notes a gradual tendency towards lighter, thinner work. The simplest ornament in such a stem consists of air drawn down from

59. Smoothly rounded drinking glasses decorated only by subdued
acid-etching from the renowned Northwood workshop, Wordsley, *c.* 1870.
Broadfield House Glass Museum, Kingswinford.

the base of the bowl into a tear or long, ill-shaped bubble. An interesting rarity is the so-called Excise glass with a stem blown as a hollow tube to reduce the glass's weight.

In Chapter Five I described the making of incised twist stems and the more widely popular air-twists, opaque enamel twists, colour twists and composite stems that brought a new charm to this straight-stemmed Georgian glassware with white or coloured spirals covered in clear glass. Here especially was brilliant outpouring of skill, keeping British glassmen in the forefront of their craft. Air-twists, first introduced in two-piece glasses, became more exact and intricate when the stem was made separately. 'Worm'd glasses' were being advertised even before 1740; but Bernard Hughes has drawn attention to the flaws that can be found in early pre-1750 twists. Soon, however, glassmen even found it possible to introduce knops in order to display the internal twists more brilliantly, often as shoulder knops, but sometimes as central swellings and occasionally as a series of knops down the stem. Opaque white twist stems, too, may be found with knopped shaping, but comparatively rarely, perhaps from consideration of cost: from 1777 even the white enamel itself was subject to tax.

Collectors date the important periods for twist stems as follows: incised twists and air twists, c. 1740 to 1770; opaque white, mixed air and opaque, and colour twists c. 1750 to 1780; composite stems, (plain and twist sections) c. 1745 to 1775.

Some collectors, of course, find these brilliantly clever twist stems as naive as sticks of seaside rock. They applaud instead the lightly wheel-cut ornament that links another group of this period's drinking glasses under the classification of facet-cut stems. The main fashion for these extraordinarily attractive stems is usually considered to have started in the 1760s although with at least occasional earlier examples. Some collectors prefer to trace their rise to popularity from c. 1780, when glass could be more successfully annealed and when untaxed Irish glass became an important source.

On bowls, especially in the thicker glass expected of vessels for dry sweetmeats, early cutting included large diamond and triangular shapes in extremely low relief (so called flat cutting or slice cutting). However, by facet-cutting the collector implies close, regular arrangements of shallow scoops ground into the glass surface, such as diamond shapes, hexagons, rounded flutes or scales. (Vertical flutes are associated with the 1800s.) These are pleasing to the fingers and produced a shimmering reflective brilliance through a period when table glass shared with silver and Sheffield plate in reflecting the many-candled splendour of important social occasions, only less brilliant than the massed diamonds and gold of the company's flaunting jewellery.

Such facets or shallow flutes frequently encircle the bowl's base, linking bowl and stem in a harmonious flowing line and being known as bridge fluting. This particularly well suits the ogee-shaped bowl and indeed faceted stems are mainly associated with such bowls and those in similar rounded funnel and ovoid outlines, then ousting thistle and bell shapes. Sometimes the bowl shows engraving, but the collector may look with suspicion on a

79

60. Wine glasses with ovoid bowls linked to the faceted stems by bridge fluting. Centre-left has a circuit of seven facets instead of the usual six and below the semi-knop a circuit of hexagonal facets gives the stem a slight swelling. Centre-right, the oval facets on the bowl are matched on the foot.

glass combining a mould-patterned bowl with a facet-cut stem.

As to the stem outlines, at their simplest they may be straight-cut hexagonal columns or notched with horizontal ridges. It is more usual to find this hexagonal stem cut all over with closely placed long-diamond slices, elaborated only with an occasional shoulder knop or a central pointed knop in a particularly satisfying cusped effect. Facet cutting coincided with a liking for stems that were slightly shorter than those with twist ornament.

Clearly when the glass-cutter worked on the bowl and stem of the finished glass he would be expected to smooth down the disfigurement of the pontil mark and the feet of these glasses tended to be made flatter in consequence. They are most often plain, although occasionally the rim is scalloped with a slanting edge, or domed and facet-cut. (Such niceties, of course, are most often associated with the smaller feet of luxury sweetmeat glasses that would come under close scrutiny on the dessert table).

One other style of drinking glass requires mention in this early-to-mid-Georgian chapter although it appeared in full splendour mainly around the end of the century. This is the rummer, a general-purpose goblet now too closely associated with rum punch. It is conspicuously different in that here once more the stem has become of minor importance, and dating must depend mainly upon features of bowl and foot.

Few have survived from the early 18th century but many survive from the later part of that century demonstrating that the style was popular by the 1760s when this ancient Graeco-Roman shape (associated too with Elizabethan glass) suited the period's neo-classical vogue and might be engraved with the familiar 'Adam' motifs such as circuits of laurel, swags and bell flowers.

The ovoid bowl, a deeply rounded egg-cup shape, tapered into a short drawn stem on a substantial foot. Many were of rough tavern quality, but others offered wonderful scope for wheel-engraving. They covered a wide range of sizes, but survivors suggest that capacities of four to eight ounces were popular. The short stem below the large bowl lowered the centre of gravity permitting use of a relatively small foot.

Among the finest rummers of the 1770s were those with hollow flutes encircling the bowl—repeated later in blown-moulded glasses. The drawn stem was expanded into a dome shape for attaching to the round foot, which measured about two-thirds the diameter of the bowl. Some feet were flat, some still conical—still shielding pontil scars.

Among other minor groups of almost stemless glasses at this period was the short ale flute. This continued in the style described in Chapter Six. By the 1770s to 1780s the tall funnel bowl might rest on a brief stem characterised by one or more flattened angular knops above a wide, sometimes folded, foot. Short-stemmed drams continued, acquiring somewhat more character when given the massive foot required of a firing glass (Chapter Thirteen).

Influenced to some extent by the 1745 *Excise Act*, but also probably by the general style of these glasses, feet in the 1740s tended to be made plain—without the strength and weight of folded-under rims, although these continued on less fashionable glass as late as the 1830s. Domed feet, too became rare but the pontil mark by its continuing presence ensured that the usual shape was still an attractive low cone. The only exception was the heavy foot required for the table-rapping associated with firing glasses, as described in Chapter Thirteen.

Collectors usually find little difficulty in distinguishing their drinking glasses from the stemmed dessert glasses intended

61. Heavy-footed firing glasses with rare opaque twist stems. Inscribed
KING-QUEEN-ROYAL-FAMILY and THE KING AND THE FRIENDS OF HIS
MAJESTY'S AMERICAN LOYALISTS, *c.* 1765.

for 'wet sweetmeats' such as custard and jelly, which often had delicate double (B-shape) handles. Different again are the 18th century's footed tankards, most usually found in the silversmith's slightly waisted style, very often with a band of applied stringing around the rim and a gadrooned base above a small moulded foot. The characteristic handle is a loop turned out at the base into a jaunty s-shape. Handleless thick-based tumblers are found too, including the highly prized Norwich or Lynn style with horizontal corrugations.

CHAPTER NINE

Late Georgian Decanters
1790s to 1830s

REGENCY IN SPIRIT if not exactly in time, the years from *c.* 1790 to the 1830s saw comparatively few changes in decanter shapes, but a spectacular change in the ornament they might bear. From the reticence in engraved and cut patterns associated with the 1790s glassmen progressed to the most flamboyant splendour expected of the power-assisted glass-cutter in late-Georgian days with shape becoming subordinate to deep-cut geometrical patterns devised to maximise their glitter in flickering candlelight.

As Hugh Wakefield has noted in *Nineteenth Century British Glass*:

> British glass factories were on the point of exerting their greatest influence on the world history of glass. . . . It was in the early decades of the 19th century that they perfected their style of cutting in the manner in which it achieved its widest international popularity and in which it has survived to the present day as a well-respected tradition.

This led to the development of French and Belgian glass-works, widespread imitation in the United States and failure in Venice.

Much glassware, of course, came from English glassmen working in Ireland, taking advantage of the tax freedom to create massive, thick-walled vessels to the delight of the glass-cutter, although some commentators have exaggerated their contribution. (*See* Chapter Fourteen.) The style reflects the spirit of its day with superb traditional craftsmanship unceasingly challenged by technical advance. In Britain at this time those who could afford it sought reassurance in ever more substantial pompous splendour, culminating in the florid grandeur of the 1820s to 1830s whether urbane as Paul Storr silver or gauche as Rockingham rhinoceros vases.

This was the period of the huge suite of matching decanters and drinking glasses, sometimes numbered in hundreds, at the mercy of a wild night's drinking party. I have referred already to the fitted cabinets of squares and glasses fashionable through Regency and early Victorian days.

83

62. (*Left*) Neo-classical decanters on stepped square pedestal feet, 1790s.

63. (*Right*) Prussian shape decanters finely engraved with the ship *Susanna* among fruiting vines, *c.* 1790s.

Armorial services were especially prized. One for the Marquess of Londonderry made by the Wear Flint-Glass Company in 1824 consisted of 24 covers (including, for example, four sizes of wine glasses), totalled over 500 pieces and cost 2,000 guineas. In general outline the decanters of this period tended to become broader and heavier, with shorter, thicker necks and squarer shoulders, wide-lipped and with heavily finialed stoppers. The Prussian shape, with sloping shoulders and somewhat inward-slanting to the base, named and illustrated by John Keeling of Dudley in 1784, was a long-favoured alternative to the stave-and-hoop-marked barrel described in Chapter Seven. Many were mould-blown with the lower part of the body ribbed or comb-fluted. More costly free-blown hand-cut examples were in thicker glass and in the 1790s to 1800s might be engraved, sometimes with a crest or monogram on one side and a motif of personal interest on the other, but often merely with an encircling repeat pattern.

Neck-rings, tentatively introduced on taper and early barrel decanters in the 1780s, became expected details on the Prussian, with two, or more often three, equally spaced down the widening neck below a substantial and somewhat wider brim. The rings were applied one by one by dropping a thread of hot molten glass on to

FALCON GLASS WORKS, Holland Street, Blackfriars' Road, London.

APSLEY PELLATT'S

ABRIDGED LIST OF

Net Cash Prices for the best Flint Glass Ware.

DECANTERS.

25 Strong quart Nelson shape decanters, cut all over, bold flutes and cut brim & stopper, P.M. each 10s6d. to 12 0

26 Do. three-ringed royal shape, cut on and between rings, turned out stop, P.M. each 10 0
    Do. do. not cut on or between rings, nor turned out stopper, P.M. ea. 8s to 9 0

27 Fancy shapes, cut all over, eight flutes, spire stopper, &c. each, P.M. 16s. to 18 0
    Do. six flutes only, each, P.M. 24s. to 27 6

DISHES.

31 Dishes, oblong, pillar moulded, scolloped edges, cut star.

5-in.	7-in.	9-in.	10-in.
3s. 6d.	6s. 6d.	11s.	13s. each.

64. Excerpt from Apsley Pellatt price list illustrating Nelson and royal shape decanters, 1830s.

the reheated vessel as it was rotated by the gaffer at his chair. After more heating at the glory hole the rings were pinched to shape with a spring tool. It was usual for them to match each other, although collectors note a considerable range of style through this period, from the simple rounded outline, sometimes doubled or trebled, to angular shaping, 'feathered' or herringbone decoration, with rows of opposing slanted cuts and the more elaborate patterns that arrived when deep-cut diamond ornament gave the whole luxury decanter its later Georgian sparkle.

Apsley Pellatt's 'Falcon Flint-Glass and Steam Cutting Works', London, made a feature of the cut brim and turned-out stopper (with a tall stem fanning out into a flattish mushroom cap) on their long-popular 'Nelson' decanter. This had 'bold flutes' on neck and body with only a single rounded neck-ring but their 'three-ringed royal shape' was distinguished by decorative cutting both on and between the rings, accounting for a shilling or more of the price (10 shillings).

Usually the 'late Regency' decanter had an angular shoulder line where neck met body, giving a crisper silhouette than that of the Prussian and becoming a feature of decanters with cylindrical or only very slightly tapering bodies. These were sometimes known

85

as drum shaped when kettle-drum bowls were popular with the Irish glasshouses. They continued until the 1840s. The outline lent itself especially to the wide vertical fluting and heavy reeding of the 1820s to 1830s which might be contrasted with horizontal prismatic cutting around the broad neck.

Stopper finials in the 1790s, plain, cut or pinched in hand presses, most often continued the flat vertical disc outlines of the 1780s, such as the circular target and bull's-eye with a central hollow or boss on each face, and the inverted pear outline. Popular Regency details included radiating ridges around the central boss and a serrated edge. But *c.* 1800 the liking for horizontal emphasis in all design was expressed even in this decanter detail and the mushroom shape well suited the somewhat dumpy round-shouldered Prussian decanter.

The mushroom was usually flat on its underside, but with its low dome grooved to suggest radiating gadroons. This finial might stand well above the decanter brim, more or less equalling its diameter on a straight or knopped stem, above the usual tapering stopper. A more massive hollow deep-cut variant persisting into the 1840s suggested diminishing discs laid above and below a substantial cushion. Sometimes the mushroom was rounded into a hemisphere and occasionally a ball shape, hollow or solid, with relief diamond patterning. In the 1820s tall pinnacle finials appeared too.

It is interesting to find a number inconspicuously engraved under or on the edge of the brim of a finely cut decanter and a corresponding figure on the base of its matching stopper, indicating a successful attempt to ensure the close fit of a stopper ground to suit the individual vessel. But this is rare and the collector must accept that decanters would often be fitted with stoppers from outside suppliers, using perhaps a slightly different quality of glass. It was an item often supplied cheaply to the glasshouse by the specialist pinchers mentioned in Chapter Four. In any case such a vulnerable item must often be a replacement. The important consideration is that its style should be in keeping with the decanter's supposed date and, equally important, that the finial and not just the stopper should be of appropriate size.

For most collectors, however, as for their original owners, the main attraction of all these decanters lies in their decoration. This

65 (*Left*) Extensive diamond cutting on Regency decanters including diamond-cut neck-rings and fine diamonds around the base separated by flutes and printies.
66. (*Right*) Regency water carafe – with simple wide and narrow flute cutting most effective on brilliant flint-glass.

developed as restrained patterns of shallow geometrical cutting gave place to the deep cutting that was developed gradually in the early 19th century to display lead-rich flint-glass in full flamboyant splendour. I describe some of the most popular patterns in Chapter Five, but collectors find almost endless variety in the arrangement of the straight and mainly v-profile (mitre) cuts that appeared especially in the parallel lines of prism cutting, the radiating lines of star cutting and the parallel intersections that created fields of relief and fine diamonds. A typical design of the 1820s might have horizontal prismatic cutting low on the neck with vertical flutes to the shoulder, then more prismatic cutting to edge a wide band of hobnail or other diamonds forming the main body ornament and with vertical or slanting blazes above the base. But some decanters were merely cut with horizontal prisms throughout.

By the late 1820s to 1830s, however, the most important decorative detail was probably the wide shallow vertical flute, attuned to the cylindrical decanter. Even neck-rings lost favour because they interfered with the new emphasis on vertical lines. A hint of the problems facing the men who wheel-cut these heavy vessels is indicated by Apsley Pellatt who charged 16 shillings to 18 shillings for a decanter cut from spire stopper to base in eight flutes but 24 shillings to 27 shillings for one with only six, much wider, flutes. In the 1830s, a period associated with sprawling 'revived rococo' patternings in other home furnishings, even conservative glass-cutters introduced groups of printies and other rounded motifs.

Apsley Pellatt himself enlivened the sides and finials of some decanters with the *cristallo ceramie* ornament described in Chapter Five. The decanter's convex body displayed the little heads and busts in silvery china clay to particular advantage, and surroundings of deep cutting masked slight thickening of the clear glass necessary to enclose them. In his book *Curiosities of Glassmaking* Pellatt referred to these incrustations in decanters and wine glasses and the 'superb effect when enclosed in richly cut glass'. More were made by John Ford & Company of Edinburgh in the 1870s.

Throughout this period an alternative to increasingly lavish cutting was the use of coloured glass, rich blue or now rarer deep green. This was deployed with spectacular effect in Bohemia and South-east Germany – including the use of heavily opaque hyalith and lithyalin – partly as a reaction against the British success with leaded flint-glass which appeared to flash fire from every sharply cut detail. In England coloured glass met only a minor demand, however, and it too might be cut with flat diamonds, fluting and the like. Some fine decanters appeared in the 1820s in a rich purplish blue coloured with post-war supplies of refined Saxon cobalt. The colour was named king's blue when George IV showed his pleasure in a coronation gift of a gilded blue glass spirit set – a large oval tray holding three labelled decanters and a dozen glasses.

Gilding was particularly effective – while it lasted – on a decanter's facted ball stopper-finial and wide brim, as well as being useful for labelling the contents. Typically, three green glass spirit decanters in the Victoria and Albert Museum labelled for brandy, rum and hollands (gin) have corresponding initial letters in gilt on their faceted ball finials, gilt rings on their short necks and further gilding to suggest the staves and hoops on their barrel-shaped bodies.

Gilded labels from such workshops as those of Lazarus and Isaac Jacobs, active 1771 to 1806, mentioned in Chapter Five, had long lost their mid-Georgian flourished style of presentation and the wine or spirit names are usually found in the Regency's favourite plain outline, a clipped-corner rectangle. More adventur-.ous use of colour, such as the casing tentatively introduced in the 1830s, is so much a part of Victorian glass that it is considered in Chapter Eleven.

Coloured glass – blue, green, amber and red – is found too, in some of the mould-blown decanters and squares made after the invention of open-and-shut moulds as described in Chapter Four. This gave the less affluent a chance to spread their tables with handsome glassware. Obviously mould-blown glass had to imitate deep cutting; the ribbings, flutings and diamond diapers orna-menting such vessels – less sharp than hand-cutting – have their own subtle light effects, due to the corresponding interior undula-tions. After c. 1835 even the neck brim might be included in the mould shaping. Stoppers might be mould-blown or 'pinched' in solid glass – mushroom, target, steeple or ball.

Roman pillar moulding was a cheap strong form of ornament for such vessels as carafes, patented in 1835 by Thomas Green and licensed to others. Although this was a mould-blown process and the vessel's exterior was heavily gadrooned, the interior was almost smooth. Such ornament may be found combined with cut fluting. Hugh Wakefield notes this use of 'heavy protruding elements' as an international trend, found also in heavy gadrooning and in-dentations, from mushroom stopper finial to wine glass foot.

Among other vessels on the late Georgian dining-table the col-lector looks for a claret jug, probably matching a pair of decanters, with a wide spout, plain handle and circular foot. Ornate silver-mounted claret jugs (safer than those with glass handles) became increasingly favoured through the century. Another dinner-table vessel was the stopperless 'water craft' or carafe, mentioned in Chapter Seven. A rarity here is the carafe in two sections, silver-mounted to unscrew below the shoulder. This is thought to have been a bedroom vessel, so made to facilitate cleaning when used for a popular medicinal wine, cinchona, which stained the glass. A more interesting curiosity, suggesting at first glance a wide-based decanter, was the fly or wasp catcher. This was raised on three shell or ball feet and instead of a base the bottom rim curved inward to form an encircling two-inch trough or gutter. This was filled with sweetened ale, attracting insects which drowned.

CHAPTER TEN

Late Georgian Glasses

1790s to 1830s

Around the end of the 18th century and on through Regency and late-Georgian days, drinking glasses, like decanters, illustrated the great effects of technical advance. Better annealing permitted the deeper, more extravagant cut ornament demanded by the rich, while mould-blown vessels from full-size two-part and three-part moulds met the ever-increasing demands of everyone else. But most of us probably associate this period especially with engraved ornament on rummer and flute, tankard and tumbler, recording so many hopes and pleasures of those uproarious days.

A price list of the Rotherham Glass Works included wines, flutes, hock glasses, goblets (all sizes), drams (priced with poor quality wines) sham-drams and tumblers. The sham-dram with a deceptive bowl has been mentioned in Chapter Three. A new name for it in late-Georgian and Victorian days was the joey, called after the new silver fourpenny piece introduced in 1836. The bowl should have held fourpennyworth of gin, but in fact half that quantity filled it to the brim.

Drams in an 1811 price list from Glasgow might be ribbed, sham or thick. The Edinburgh and Leith Glasshouse introduced the thistle shape at this time. However, with the return to more gin drinking from the late 1820s great numbers of glasses were made in crude tumbler form, two or three inches tall with thick ribbed bases and out-curving rims.

Wine glasses contributed little of great interest, their bowls continuing in ovoid, bucket and rounded-funnel outlines, but by the 1830s tending to show less generous and more curving outlines such as slender trumpet and waisted ogee. Wide flat facets or shallow-cut bridge-fluting around the lower half of the bowl might link bowl and stem, extending far up the sides by the 1820s. But many bowls were plain and some conventionally engraved. All tended to be short-stemmed. Stem facets gradually became less popular than vertical fluting, which was often introduced above

67. (*Left*) Designs from the pattern book of the Edinburgh and Leith Glass Company, *c.* 1811. Top: heavy rummers on round or square pedestal feet and with deep diamond cutting and vertically fluted stems. Below: tall champagne flutes on wide feet.

68. (*Right*) Cider flute engraved with sprays of rose, thistle and shamrock, the bowl drawn into a heavy, twisted stem on a plain foot; height 14½ ins; early 19th century.

and below a central knop, perhaps facet-cut. This fluting continued into early Victorian days and more knops variously shaped and cut came back into favour in the 1820s. Feet were usually plain, occasionally decorated with sliced or radial cutting.

Deep flute glasses, with funnel, rounded-funnel and elongated ovoid bowls, are associated with this period, for ales, cider and champagne—although champagne itself was rarely seen in England from the 1790s until after 1815. An 1817 list included flutes in fifteen styles and sizes. The continuing popularity of short and dwarf ale flutes has already been referred to. A stemmed flute, six or seven inches tall, might have a plain drawn stem; more often a fluted bowl, cut or moulded, had a stem with a central knop in bladed, ball or other outline, sometimes faceted, and there might be a shoulder knop too. Feet might be plain or folded.

The Rotherham Glassworks as late as 1829 still included 'cyders purled' to mask the sediment, as described in Chapter Six and 'cyders with twisted stems and welted feet'. A twelve-inch flute with its three-inch stem twisted into half-a-dozen wide spirals can be a splendid vessel, well suited to commemorative engraving.

For the sparkling champagne of the 1830s fashion approved a hemispherical bowl on a tall thin stem and small foot.

The goblets generally known as rummers are a delight to collect. They continue the general style described in Chapter Eight with a deep ovoid bowl on a short stem, frequently knopped, and a small foot; included are many a plain bowl roundly tapering into a short drawn stem for the tavern keeper. About 1800 the bowl might be bucket-shaped, with its straight sides vertical or slightly inward sloping; also, by then, the flat base of the bowl was more attractively linked to the stem by a disc, with round or bladed edge.

The heavy foot, still continuing to measure less in diameter than the bowl rim, was at its most attractive when shaped as a domed square plinth, hollowed and ridged on the underside—now often known as the lemon-squeezer shape—but this was a short-lived extravagance. Round feet too might be cut or moulded underneath, in star pattern, this becoming frequent in the 1820s.

The large-capacity serving, or toddy, rummer with a deep-cup bowl, too large for comfortable drinking, was strengthened with a collar at the bowl junction. The short stem was spread widely to attach to the flattish foot—for a vessel intended for serving hot toddy had to be sturdily built throughout. As deep cutting became widely popular the circuit of broad fluting around the base of the goblet bowl was supplemented occasionally by bands of diamond-cutting, prism-cutting and the like, decorating but not yet overwhelming the vessel shape. Many bowls were engraved.

These gave an opportunity for the commemorative scenes and propaganda considered in Chapter Thirteen. But many glasses also have delightfully personal themes. Sports are recorded and scenes

69. (*Left*) Rummer engraved with a toast to the *David*, with a square pedestal base hollowed and ridged on the underside, now often known as a lemon squeezer base, early 19th century.

70. (*Right*) Simple toddy rummer typical of tavern glass around the turn of the century. Engraved in diamond point with its owner's name, Edward Giles of the Cross Keys, Heath Town, Wolverhampton; 1790s. Below is a toddy drinker's glass sugar crusher.

of travel, and many more vessels are associated with long-forgotten local societies or wish success to trades or ships or the humble plough. Even when the main motif is merely a flourished monogram the engraver has usually added something on the reverse.

Associated in name, but not in style, the early roemer returned at this time, with its distinctive incurving bowl and wide stem (occasionally hollow as noted below by the *Pottery Gazette*) and with protruding prunts. This hock glass, illustrated for example among the Edinburgh and Leith Glass Company's patterns of *c.* 1816, might still be made in traditional green-toned glass. 'Hock glasses threaded and prunted' cost one shilling more than wine glasses, the glass threading wound closely around the domed foot.

Following the bowl styles of this period's flutes and goblets was the vessel now generally known as a coaching glass, a footless vessel such as had long served the passing horseman wishing to drink a stirrup cup. This is considered in Chapter Three and it is enough here to remind collectors to be on their guard against normal glasses converted into such vessels after foot damage.

This period especially favoured stemless glasses, such as tumblers, tankards and mugs. J. A. Brooks has drawn attention to a detail regarding handled vessels, suggesting a date of *c.* 1860 for a change in the way that the handle was applied: earlier, the handle was attached first at the top of the vessel; later the base of the handle was applied first, to ensure greatest strength for lifting.

Regency and late Georgian tumblers were short, with thick bases, becoming taller in mid-Victorian days. The slanting sides were straight or slightly curved, with characteristic wide fluting up to half height or more. An 1830 record of trade in the Midlands and North reviewed in the *Pottery Gazette* in 1899 noted that the tumblers illustrated were chiefly 'plain, fluted, flutes and splits and in a few cases edge-flutes and balls', with some engraving. All the wines had solid stems except two, 'and one of these is what we should call a "claret" or hock . . . Tumblers fetched from 16s. to 24s. per dozen. Wines from 9s. 6d. to 15s.' Apsley Pellatt advertised no fewer than ten nearly similar designs for vertically fluted and reeded tumblers; his patented cameo incrustations (described in Chapter Five) were particularly effective when decorating a set of matching tumblers, surrounded by deep cutting in his brilliantly clear flint-glass. Rotherham Glassworks in 1829 made no mention of tankards, but priced tumblers by their capacity, adding that on a moulded tumbler a star or ornamental bottom added an extra twopence per pound weight. Tumblers were also among the first vessels to be made in the 1840s in the pressed glass that dominated this cheaper market through Victorian days.

At the most popular–even peasant art–level the collector may find mugs and tumblers and occasional handled serving bottles among so-called Nailsea glass. For a time around the beginning of the 19th century a number of glass centres produced simple domestic ware, such as flasks and mugs, in this lightly taxed unrefined dark brownish-green bottle glass, attractively flecked and striped with white or rarer coloured enamel (often now crazed). Vessels in clearer pale green glass may be found dating from perhaps 1810 onwards.

CHAPTER ELEVEN

Victorian Innovations

VICTORIAN GLASS came to life in 1845. Excise duty was abolished and with it the 'dead hand' of the men who had had to watch and weigh the glassmen's every enterprising notion. But this is such a tremendously rich period in British glass history on every level, from superb to better-forgotten, that it is easiest perhaps to review it in three periods: early Victorian, up to the Great Exhibition or the early 1850s; high Victorian, 1850s to 1870s; late Victorian, late 1870s onwards with, of course, inevitable overlapping.

In the Stourbridge area alone, Thomas Webb & Sons recorded over 25,000 Victorian patterns and this was but one of the region's many successful firms whose work is brilliantly displayed at Broadfield House, Kingswinford, a major glass museum in the

71. Cut glass. Left: *c.* 1850. Left-centre and centre: probably Richardson work, late 19th century. Right-centre and right: Stevens & Williams, late 19th century, that on the right being 'brilliant cut' (rock crystal glass). Broadfield House Glass Museum, Kingswinford.

Metropolitan Borough of Dudley, organised by Mr Charles Hajdamach. Throughout the period, conservative work in clear uncoloured glass was rivalled by specifically Victorian techniques that introduced intriguing new ways with colour and the press-shaping that became a feature of glassworks in the North-East. This spectacular period also witnessed important developments in the whole conception of art-glass manipulation and chemistry, importantly influenced by Harry Powell of London's Whitefriars Glasshouse.

Always, as in other home furnishings, the collector must beware of the Victorians' self-distrusting affection for the styles approved by previous centuries, shown in a succession of supposedly revived-rococo, neo-Gothic, Elizabethan, Jacobean and neo-classical shapes and motifs that are misleading rather than true to the originals. Indeed the collector may consider a possible Victorian origin for any glass that nearly – but not quite – fits the trend of an earlier period. Equally important, was the Victorians' continuing admiration for the wonders of early Venice – with brittle soda-glass delicacies interpreted, of course, in lustrous flint-glass.

To begin, then, with early Victorian mainstream table glass in clear flint-glass, decanter bodies in the 1840s emphasised the late-Georgian liking for massive cylinder shapes. Engraved ornament continued, of course, but the main interest was in very heavy cutting of large geometrical motifs additionally weighted with such protuberances as pillar mouldings and the gadroons associated too with some drinking-glass bowls.

The revived-rococo liking for curves soon suggested a greater freedom of pattern, however, from rows of printies to neo-Gothic arches, and around the mid-century a decanter's shape might recall the Jacobean shaft-and-globe, or the contemporary china jug outline of over-long neck widening into a plump, sagging body on a wide foot.

From this the obvious high-Victorian change was to footed neo-classical urn or pear and inverted pear outlines. Late-Georgian straight-sided shapes lingered on only in tall jugs for ale or fruit drinks: these, as in 1860s pottery, might be nearly cylindrical, widening only a little towards the base.

For very many years from the 1870s one of the most favoured shapes for decanter and claret jug followed the Greek potter's

72. (*Left*) Engraving of a claret jug, shaft-and-globe decanter, straight-sided, wide-footed water jug, stemmed glasses and tumbler, by A. Pellatt, W. Naylor and J. G. Green, shown at the Great Exhibition, 1851.

73. (*Right*) Claret jug in oenochoe shape, with a trefoil mouth, long slender neck, ovoid body and small foot, suitably enriched with finely engraved ornament in classic style. Broadfield House Glass Museum, Kingswinford.

oenochoe with a trefoil mouth above a long neck on an ovoid body and small flat foot. By then other decanters including handled vessels for warm claret had rounded bodies, shorter necked, but with tall-stemmed ball-finial stoppers, a frequent finial detail being a tiny knop on top. The handle in the 1860s to 1870s became a somewhat clumsy decorative feature, closely ribbed down to a massive claw-like base gripping the vessel's shoulder. I refer in Chapter Ten to the way that the handle was attached to jug or tankard.

The oenochoe was essentially a thin-blown graceful outline and a feature of high-Victorian glass was the near abandonment of deep cutting from the 1850s until it was restored to elegant high fashion

in the 1880s. If reasons are needed for such a change, there was the general exuberance of 1840s glass with critics of the time quick as always to condemn English manufacture: the 1851 Exhibition Jury deplored many 'errors of taste'. But many practical glass-cutters must have thought their craft doomed anyway by the development of passable imitations in cheap press-patterned glass for the main market among the rising middle classes.

This meant that traditionalists in the 1860s to 1880s concentrated on engraved ornament and collectors trace their decanter patterns through a succession of 'Elizabethan' arabesques, naturalistic flowers and the 1860s obsession with fern fronds, to figure scenes – sporting, classical and genre – and slight acknowledgements of new-found Japanese art in birds among fruit blossom. But this is to over-simplify. As I have indicated all too briefly in Chapter Five, wheel-engraving became extremely elaborate on many a high-Victorian decanter and claret jug, including the particularly pleasing deeply engraved and highly polished work known as rock crystal engraving from the late 1870s. This brilliant ornament on deliberately heavy 'lumpy' shapes is associated especially with the Stourbridge area where many engravers worked to the commission of London dealers. Bohemian immigrants William Fritsche, 1853–

74. (*Left*) Group of glasses (tumblers and
rummer) designed by Philip Webb
(1831–1915) for William Morris and made by
James Powell, *c.* 1860. Victoria and Albert
Museum, London.

75. (*Right*) Typical glass made by the
Whitefriars Glassworks (James Powell &
Sons) in late Victorian and Edwardian days.
Here the tapering ribbed body is balanced by
the wrythen stopper finial. Victoria and
Albert Museum, London.

1924, and the Kny family for example had their own workshops on
the premises of Thomas Webb & Sons. There is a fine 'Elgin'
claret jug by F. E. Kny in the Fitzwilliam Museum. Many designs
are included in the pattern books from the 1870s by the firm of
Stevens & Williams (Royal Brierley Crystal).

Such decoration was rivalled of course by late Victorian (and
Edwardian) deep cutting, more precisely exact and brilliant than
ever in heavily finialed decanters and the squares with faceted ball
stopper finials which were required for locking in the showy
tantalus frame. Through high- and late-Victorian days, however,
many 'purists' disassociated themselves from all cutting and even
much engraving. Some glasses reputedly designed by architect
Philip Webb for William Morris, *c.* 1860, now in the Victoria and
Albert Museum are plain save for wide horizontal ribbing; these
glasses show how dull the purists' alternatives might be when they
required only the limpid beauty of shape without ornament.

Ruskin's familiar pronouncement in *The Stones of Venice* on the
barbarity of all cut glass, because ductility was concealed, merely
gave a rallying cry to those intellectuals. More interesting is the
comment by Harry Powell that cutting aimed 'to give expression
to one of the essential qualities of glass, namely its inherent

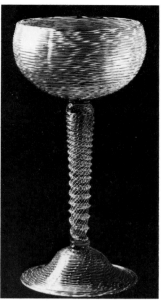

76. (*Left*) A water jug with water lilies painted in enamels; by the firm of W. H., B. & J. Richardson of Wordsley, Stourbridge. Marked RICHARDSON'S VITRIFIED and with a Patent Office Design Registry mark for 1848. Victoria and Albert Museum, London.

77. (*Right*) Coupe of blue-green striped with white and covered with trailing. This won a prize in a Society of Arts competition, 1869–70. Made by Joseph Leicester at James Powell & Sons; height 8½ ins. Victoria and Albert Museum, London.

brilliancy . . . without obscuring or cloaking the form given by the glassblower's breath'. For Powell was the late-Victorian intellectuals' hero and is remembered for such vessels as decanters in superbly graceful slender outlines, decorated, if at all, with such details as delicate ribbing and surface trailing. His remarkable skills in glass designed for shaping and decorating at the furnace mouth won him recognition as the equal of any glassman in Europe.

In his *Glassmaking in England* Powell illustrated a 'flat shaped hollow-sided claret bottle' with glass trailing on finial and neck, and also a 'poppy head' decanter (with a similar finial) and with a fluted neck and 'four deep dents in the body' to provide a secure grip, both *c*. 1880. These were designed to dispense with the need for the vulnerable handle on the heated claret vessel—as an alternative to ornate silver harness. Two other Powell illustrations are of subtly curving decanters slightly wheel-engraved with swirling lines.

Tall tapering vessels were then high fashion, the ball stopper finial rising on a long stem above a narrow brim, plain or frilled, the neck nearly as long as the body (longer on the late version of the shaft-and-globe) the body often in pear or inverted pear shape, usually footed and still reminiscent of the oenochoe.

Much use was made of simple base fluting, circuits of stars, richly cut or thinly etched, and other minor conventional ornament, such as round or oval printies then known as mirrors or thumbprints. However, even fashionable Harrods in 1895 noted a 'growing demand for Plain Table Glass'. A typical suite then contained 87 pieces: 12 each of glasses for sherry, port, claret, champagne and of tumblers and finger basins, 6 liqueur glasses, 2 carafes and tumblers, 2 quart decanters, 2 pint decanters and 1 for claret. Newly-weds were glad enough to receive what was known as a cabaret set containing decanter or claret jug matched to a pair of goblets.

Victorian drinking glasses are equally difficult to classify. Here again the early period saw the change from somewhat squat squarish forthright vessels with vertical facets or flutes to a bewildering variety of shapes, dated to some extent by the changes in ornament described for their accompanying decanters. Inevitably they include such obvious revivals as baluster and enamel-twist stems. However, the baluster swellings might now be concentrated towards the foot, in the 1840s' dowdy outline, the waisted stems too showily slender, and the colour twists perhaps given a 'Venetian' double loop to prove how skilful the craft had become.

As with decanters, the shapes became more rounded, some with undulating bowl silhouettes, and eventually included the slender upthrusting flower outlines associated with end-of-century art nouveau. Cutting and engraving matched them to contemporary decanters. Collectors are reminded of the technical change from pontil to gadget (Chapter Four) that resulted in many glasses being given almost flat feet.

In this brief review it is more useful perhaps to note the other great development in both glasses and decanters, the colour that proved particularly successful through early- and late-Victorian

78. (*Left*) Gilded water jug painted with flag irises. From the glassworks of the Richardson family, *c.* 1850. Broadfield House Glass Museum, Kingswinford.

79. (*Right*) Goblet in clear crystal cased with ruby; shown by the Richardson firm at the Great Exhibition. Broadfield House Glass Museum, Kingswinford.

days. This, at its simplest, included attractive painting on clear glass, such as the leaves and flowers of water plants on decanters and jugs–for instance by J. F. Christy (Lambeth)–commissioned by Henry Cole in the late 1840s for his hopefully taste-improving, but short-lived, Felix Summerly Art Manufactures. More flamboyant enamelled and gilded ornament followed the Bohemian style. Semi-opaque opaline glass, white or tinted, might be painted too. Its smooth or roughened surface was useless for cutting but goblets and tumblers may even be found with transfer-printed scenes.

Clear, bright colour in the glass itself was the especial delight of early-Victorian glassmen, however, and nowhere more successfully than in the West Midlands and Birmingham with Benjamin Richardson among the leaders. Wine glasses in plain colours are often found, of course, usually in ruby red, emerald and bright green, purple and shades of yellow (as these colours were too intense for much effective cutting in the early years). More imaginatively, decanters and drinking-glass bowls might be blown in several layers of different colours and opaque white fused together by heat in the casing or overlay process. Usually the innermost layer was of clear glass, so that patterns wheel-ground through the outer layers offered windows to reveal the liquor bordered by slanting edges showing the different colours.

A matching set of wine glasses could be made by blowing the coloured glass in a long tube and from it cutting the cup shapes for casing clear glass. To avoid colour difference, all such details as finials, handles, stems and feet were usually of clear uncoloured glass.

Casing in a single colour, especially red, over clear glass or more thinly applied flashing (Chapter Four), proved effective too for wheel-engraved ornament: a very fine goblet in Broadfield House Museum shows sensitive flower engraving by W. J. Muckley, chief designer for the firm of W. H., B. & J. Richardson.

Cameos in neo-classical mood were hand-carved in cased glass by John Northwood, father and son, also of the Brierley Hill, Stourbridge region. These were so greatly admired that for a time commercial cameo ornament such as flowers and vines in delicately detailed low relief appeared on table glass, but with the background removed by acid. Hence the imitative market for poor quality so-called painted cameos mainly of Victorian children at play that flooded into England from Bohemia, to become associated, for no apparent reason, with an American Mary Gregory who seemingly did no such work. Eventually, of course, these were copied everywhere.

A variant of casing produced silvered glass, patented 1849, as mentioned in Chapter Four. Such 'silver' drinking glasses are too thick and too light in the hand to be taken for metal and the shape tends to be clumsy, but when further cased with colour the metallic gleam gives a subtle brilliance to cut or engraved ornament. Some were marked by the dealer Edward Varnish.

Surface textures were important to the cool, lily-white hands of Victorian hostesses. I have referred already to the use of ribbed handles: one pleasing alternative was to twist the hot glass like the incised-twist stems mentioned in Chapter Five. More showily, decanter-stopper finials, necks and handles and the bowls and stems of drinking glasses could be covered closely with glass threading in such colours as pale ruby, 'old gold' and light blue. Benjamin Richardson patented a machine that improved the quality of this threading in the 1860s.

More simply a vessel might be dotted with little knobs of coloured glass, sometimes tooled into small raspberry prunts. But an artist such as Harry Powell could achieve effects of remarkable grace and charm by emphasising the fine lines of his clear decanters and glasses with coloured glass trailing. He noted the tendency in London:

> to disregard surface decoration but to produce table-ware, graceful and simple in form, in a series of delicately tinted glasses . . . pale green and amber, straw opal (from 1879), blue opal, amethyst, horn-colour, chameleon, sea-green and sky-blue. For a short time a transparent black found favour . . . .

The Victoria and Albert Museum has an interesting prize-winning goblet with a hemispherical bowl on a tapering stem and domed foot in blue-green glass striped with white and further ornamented with trailing. This was made in 1869 by Joseph Leicester of the Whitefriars Glasshouse, a social reformer who gave up his craft to become an MP in 1885. Another brilliant experimenter, Frederick Carder, 1863–1963, was lost to English glass-making when he went to America in 1903 (Chapter Twelve).

So much has been written about cranberry glass that collectors must surely know whether they love or hate it. In Chapter Four I have indicated the several meanings applied to the term, from the early Victorians' fine, rich cherry red to the washed-out tone thinly masking imperfections in later poor quality glass. Small liqueur decanters (now perhaps mistaken for scent bottles) may be charming–so too many drinking glasses, as well as the more familiar petal-crimped toilet wares. But far more interesting is the late-Victorian development of new techniques in glass, as in ceramics, to achieve new colours and shapes by skilled control of heat and atmospheric conditions. Even these ornamental advances found occasional expression in English table glass, as illustrated by a tall goblet of Venetian delicacy made in the Powells' White-friars Glasshouse in 1876, and now at the Victoria and Albert Museum. But more of this soap-bubble iridescence in the following chapter.

CHAPTER TWELVE

Into the 20th Century

GLASS OF THE PRESENT century offers the collector many superb individual creations in 'art glass'. As the brilliant H. J. Powell commented 'the conception of the material itself has changed'. But table-glass manufacturers triumphantly introduced much beauty of shape and texture, colour and ornament into vessels that, by definition, had to conform to the requirements of functional adaptability and quantity manufacture. The Nazeing Glass Works, Broxbourne, for instance, produces 5,000 to 6,000 glasses and tumblers a day, in a vast variety of shapes and sizes.

The early-20th-century mood was worldwide. Emile Gallé, 1846–1904, (whose Nancy factory in France continued to 1935) produced sensuous, complicated landmarks in the history of art glass, but his factory also issued more conventional art-nouveau wares such as decanters and glasses spread with his rich flower patterns in colour on frosted white. His colour brilliance was reflected from the 1890s by fellow Frenchmen like the brothers August and Antonin Daum, just as the iridescent surface sheen of much glass by American Louis Comfort Tiffany, 1848–1933, was copied by Loetz of Bohemia.

Tiffany had his own commercial art-glass studios from 1893, when an important associate was the Englishman Arthur Nash from Warwickshire. Ten years later another Englishman, Frederick Carder, 1863–1963, from the West Midlands, became the first manager of the American Steuben glassworks and later art director when this merged with the Corning Glass Company in 1918. Carder joined the Brierley Hill firm of Stevens & Williams (Royal Brierley Crystal from 1925) as a trainee-designer working under the great authority on etched glass, John Northwood. He had been widely applauded and immensely assisted here in developing his brilliant talent when, aged forty, he decided to settle in America, continuing with the craft he loved until his retirement at the age of 96. Throughout Scandinavia, too, both art glass and table wares

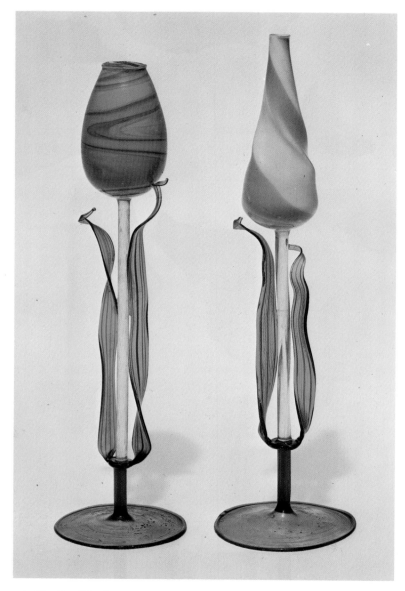

80. The English glassman's late-19th-century acknowledgement of *art nouveau*. The natural shapes of tulip buds on leaf-shrouded stems serving as small-bowled drinking glasses. Victoria and Albert Museum, London.

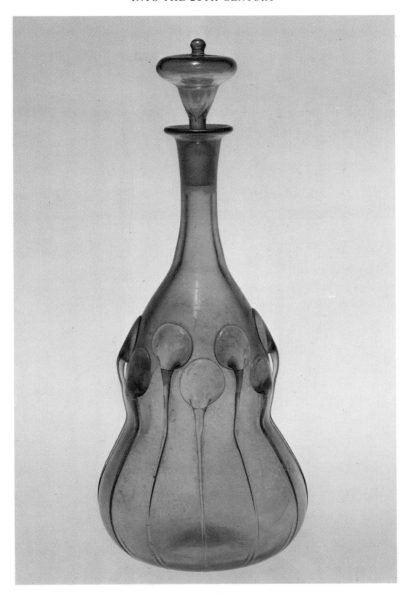

81. Iridescent favrile glass decanter with Tiffany's mark LCT; New York, 1902.
Victoria and Albert Museum, London.

82. Contemporary cut ornament in Stuart Crystal (Stuart & Sons, Stourbridge) in their Westbury pattern.

became important, most notably at Sweden's Orrefors glassworks which made a great impact at the Paris Exposition in 1937.

Table-glass design in the 1900s was still dominated by organic form in the attenuated shapes of art nouveau, with decanter and silver-mounted claret jug tapering from base to pointed finial, the occasional suggestion of up-thrusting plant growth complemented perhaps by a wavy brim. The outline was often emphasised by spiralling trails and heightened with hollowed printies. But traditional shapes continued too – the long-necked shaft-and-globe and oviform, the waisted bell and thistle and, of course, the massive round-stoppered square to fit the tantalus frame.

Ornament also tended to follow traditional lines with geometrical mitre cutting in criss-cross lines and difficult intersecting curves. In 1916 the Society of Glass Technology was founded and much table ware has continued with more restrained versions of this sought-after decoration, marvellously intricate and perfectly precise and still delighting the world with lead crystal's flashing fire.

Even table glass reflected the post-war change to the harder, sparer geometric style of art deco, but again custom demanded a certain urbane functional grace for the dinner table: it is interesting to note, in the far-ranging Royal Brierley Crystal collection, how comparatively minor have been the changes in drinking glass designs chosen by Queen Victoria and all succeeding monarchs.

The bleak art deco years are associated especially with the name of René Lalique, 1860–1945, who turned from jewellery to concentrate on glass from 1905 and was followed by his son Marc. Much of his glassware was colourless, shaped and patterned in relief with the aid of press-moulds (sometimes *cire perdue* casting) and with contrasts of polished surface and acid-frostings. Even blown decanters and drinking glasses had press-moulded necks, stems and feet. Much of the ware was of indifferent quality, but the ornament had a wide popular appeal, ranging from fly-away nymphs and cascading mimosa blossom to peacocks, fish and abstract detail, all respecting the strict rules of formalised pattern-making. He sought luminous effects rather than colour but might introduce touches of waxy red, for instance, and shining black. Collectors tend to see in it a cold worldliness perfectly reflecting the hard smart fashions of the 1920s.

Corning invited designs from Eric Gill and Sidney Waugh and many others; and in between-wars Britain too, in glass as in ceramics, professional designers were sought from outside the craft–designers as disparate as painter Dame Laura Knight (for Stuart & Sons), Clyne Farquharson (for John Walsh Walsh & Company, Birmingham) and New Zealand born architect Keith Murray, b. 1893. Murray regularly supplied designs to Royal Brierley Crystal, concentrating on simple forms firmly based and carefully proportioned in sound architectural tradition such as a best-selling decanter in a strikingly bold, angular outline. In many of his drinking glasses he placed the bowl directly upon a trumpet foot. Decoration was sparse, but ranged from flat diamond cutting to ethereal figures and sinewy fish and the period's favourite cactus.

Other notable artist designers of this period included Graham Sutherland, Paul Nash, Dod Proctor and Eric Ravilious; inevitably they lacked an inborn sympathy for their temperamental material. In contrast a West Midlands firm such as Royal Brierley Crystal can include in its museum some designs by its present Chairman, R. S. Williams-Thomas. The familiar partnership of Stevens & Williams was formed in 1846, followed by direct descendants to the present day. The firm continued making rock

83. Typical of architect Keith Murray's imaginative, finely proportioned designs in the 1930s. Royal Brierley Crystal, Brierley Hill.

crystal glass until *c*. 1930, the natural stone suggested by chunky designs in thick-walled decanters and tumblers and heavy-footed glasses, their all-over ornament deeply engraved and polished to a limpid beauty. Equally interesting was their continuing between-wars concern with colour, such as their use of cut ornament with cased glass – some triple-cased – achieving a wonderful interplay of tones by combining for example blue over cinnamon over citron over the clear crystal.

Another firm in this important West Midlands region is that of Stuart Crystal, Stourbridge, with a long family tradition stemming from 1827, when eleven-year-old orphan Frederick Stuart began his career at the Red House Glassworks. Now the fifth generation of the Stuart family controls the output of this hand-made hand-cut lead crystal including more than a dozen styles of decanter and drinking-glass services.

The Whitefriars Glassworks of James Powell and Sons moved out of London as recently as 1922. Here again craftsmanship has benefitted from long family ties with designs by Barnaby Powell, 1891–1939, recalling the pure, simple forms that made Harry Powell, 1853–1922, one of the finest glassmen in Europe. Typically

84. Magnificent rock crystal engraving on early-20th-century decanters and glasses by Stevens & Williams from *c.* 1884. Royal Brierley Crystal, Brierley Hill.

a post-war service was designed by James Hogan for our foreign embassies with the uninterrupted drop shape of the stemmed decanter echoed by the tear enclosed in each drinking-glass baluster stem.

In contrast, Dartington Glass Limited was established in Torrington, South Devon, in 1966 using Swedish expertise under Eskil Vilhelmsson as part of a concern for rural industry which has become involved still more widely in the life of the region. Many of their designs have a rugged simplicity, ranging from their wide-stemmed Regency and Bulldog services to graceful decanters and handled Gaelic coffee glasses.

Scotland's long association with glass manufacture has been noted in earlier chapters. Here too art glass caught the imagination, such as the 'primitive' bubbly Clutha glass of the 1890s made by James Couper & Sons of Glasgow where blown-glass continued until 1911, and the lustrous Monart ware introduced in 1924 by John Moncrieff of Perth Glassworks – where a particularly delicate style of table ware was given the name of muslin glass. The traditional ornamentation associated with the Edinburgh and Leith Flint Glassworks, now the Edinburgh Crystal Glass Company,

85. (*Left*) Widely different styles of modern decanter.

86. (*Right*) Victorian tavern rummer engraved by Laurence Whistler; *The Peacock Butterfly*, one of a series engraved to private commission in 1950.

continued when the firm was acquired in 1919 by Thomas Webb & Sons of Stourbridge.

When an exhibition of decorative and domestic glassware was held at Heal's, London, in 1945 the three main categories of exhibits were listed as plain glass (often coloured in green, brown or amber); glass with furnace decoration such as threads, twists and bubbles; and glass with engraved ornament.

This post-war period has come to be known by the term neo-functionalism. The emphasis was still upon suitability for purpose, but more graciously expressed, without the earlier hard angularity and benefiting from the more practical, if sometimes less imaginative, shapes and ornament provided by experienced professional industrial designers. At this time hand-cutting, restrained and graced with imaginative touches, appears to be as popular as ever; alternatives to this include hand engraving with electric-powered, free-moving tools to hold the tiny engraving-wheels, while hydro-fluoric acid may still be used to frost the glass surface with a texture that was as delicate as satin or to stipple or cut it,

87. Cumbria Crystal baluster drinking glasses from a limited edition engraved in the 'Endangered Species' series by Patrick McMahon, proceeds being donated to the World Wildlife Fund.

and, when applied with sulphuric acid, to give it a brilliant gloss.

An important development was the ornament provided by a number of clever freelance engravers, both men and women, some using diamond point and some the hand-held copper wheels. Most familiar is Laurence Whistler, b. 1912. At first he worked in diamond-point line engraving, applying his extremely personal themes to the congenial surface of fine old drinking glasses, often of the 18th century. More recently he has applied a difficult stipple technique and the glasses too are of his own design.

Today the Glass Manufacturers Federation can still list eighteen firms making stemmed drinking glasses in England, Scotland and N. Ireland, including five in the West Midlands Stourbridge area. There is some use now of a light 'lead crystal' (25 per cent lead oxide) and 'lead glass' (10 per cent) but no fewer than eleven firms still respect George Ravencroft's original formula for his lustrous 'glass of lead' and include a minimum of 30 per cent lead oxide in their 'British full lead crystal' to give our decanters and drinking glasses an incomparable sparkle.

CHAPTER THIRTEEN

Commemorative Glass

COMMEMORATIVE GLASS is uniquely challenging – and hazardous – to the beginner-collector, but wonderfully satisfying when convincingly 'right'. Drinking glasses have recorded every coronation from that of Charles II; have recalled moments of history from Culloden to Trafalgar; have lauded Liberty and Justice through many a dubious parliamentary election; and have toasted success to innumerable small groups of long-forgotten men.

Some magnificent armorial work was executed in enamels by William Beilby to commemorate the birth of an heir in 1762 (Chapter Five) and the workshop of Absolon in Yarmouth gilded many souvenirs (his subjects including a local figure of Justice). But most commemorative work was wheel-engraved (sometimes drawn in diamond-point); because one of the collector's concerns is to establish dates, both for the vessels themselves and for the motifs, these objects are particularly desirable.

All too often the motifs prove to be modern work, the lines still looking white and new, and with no subsidiary work on the reverse; often such work is crudely acid-etched. Confusingly, the glass itself may date to the 18th century when its quality well suited fine engraving. Nevertheless, a genuine commemorative vessel may show 19th-century engraving on an 18th-century glass and this may even include a 17th-century date – the year 1690 symbolically recalling the battle of the Boyne on highly prized Williamite glasses well into the 19th century.

Occasional decanters are found, but many more drinking glasses – such as bucket-bowled goblets. Tumblers of equally suitable shape for engraving included 'thumpers', so called throughout the 18th century, with very thick solid bases used for rapping the table in approval of a toast; from the 1770s they might be waisted. In time, when glass could be well annealed the vessels especially associated with such convivial occasions were short-stemmed small-capacity drams, becoming known as firing glasses

88. (*Left*) Firing glass with Masonic emblems made for Augustus Frederick, Duke of Sussex; early 19th century. Victoria and Albert Museum, London.

89. (*Right*) Jacobite glass showing a crude portrait of the Young Pretender with rose, thistle and star of hope on knopped air twist stem. Corning Museum of Glass, New York.

or masons and made far into Victorian days. Their extremely thick heavy feet were pounded on the table, making a noise likened to a volley of musketry and sometimes keeping to the regular beat known as Kentish fire. These are not to be confused with the glasses on wide, heavy feet used by officers at sea.

The field is vast but the following are among the main themes of collector-interest.

Jacobite. Support for 'James III' (James Francis Edward), the Stuart Old Pretender to the English throne, and his Young Pretender son, Charles Edward, expressed in the uprisings of 1715 and 1745.

Some collectors see early enthusiasm for the cause in the heavy baluster glass with a thistle bowl on an acorn knop stem lit by a gleaming tear. Various supportive societies and drinking groups were formed in the early 18th century such as the Cycle Club and the Sea Serjeants but most Jacobite glass post-dates 1745 when the cause was officially proscribed. Further rebellion was planned for 1750 to 1752 and glasses with not-very-secret or cryptic engraving on the bowl or under the foot were made to toast 'the king over the water'. The cause lingered on with increasing suggestions of disillusion until the death of the Old Pretender in 1766 and of his son in 1788.

Obviously the rare Jacobite glasses containing coins must be dated by their 18th-century style and quality rather than by their Stuart coins. The rest, with appropriate engraving, must be judged on merit, some perhaps having been decorated by Flemish or Dutch engravers and most coinciding with the popularity of air-twist stems. As well as crude portraits of Bonnie Prince Charlie, the many supposedly Jacobite motifs include: the heraldic rose with six or more petals, often with two buds; a star of hope; a distinctive bird resembling a jay; oak leaves; thistle; daffodil; a burgeoning oaktree stump; a moth caught in a spider's web.

Many are engraved also with Latin words or phrases such as *Fiat* (may it be so); *Radiete*, variously spelt (may he shine); *Redeat* (may he return); *Audentior Ibo* (I–the drinker–shall go more boldly). One rare group of glasses is diamond-engraved with the crowned cipher IR and verses from the paraphrase 'God Save Great James our King'. This ends 'Amen', giving the vessels the name of Amen glasses.

Anti-Jacobite. Supporters had their own secret societies such as the Calf's Head and the Muggites. Occasional glasses depict the Duke of Cumberland, commemorating his success at Culloden in 1746. Propaganda in support of George I is suggested by an occasional shouldered pedestal stem, its four sides moulded in relief with the words GOD SAVE KING GEORGE. One in the Museum of London is dated 1717. Glasses supporting the Hanoverians may be found engraved with the white rose of Hanover, the white horse of Westphalia and a toast to Liberty. King Frederick the Great of Prussia appeared on some glasses of *c.* 1757.

Williamite glasses, however, are more familiar evidence of the intensity of partisan feeling around the mid-18th century when Protestant William III's defeat of James II at the battle of the

90. (*Left*) Jacobite glass engraved with the inscription *Redeat*.
91. (*Centre*) Williamite cordial glass. Corning Museum of Glass, New York.
92. (*Right*) Privateer glass inscribed *Success to the LYON privateer*, a Bristol
based vessel of 200 tons, 44 guns and 48 men.

Boyne was widely commemorated, (indicated by the date 1690). The most attractive of these Williamite glasses, and rarer decanters, bear equestrian portraits of William. Some are engraved with the words TO THE GLORIOUS MEMORY and a few with the whole rigmarole of a toast

To the Glorious, Pious and Immortal Memory of the great and good King William who freed us from Pope and Popery Knavery and Slavery Brass Money and Wooden Shoes and may he who Refuses this toast be damned crammed and rammed down the great Gun of Athlone.

Bernard Hughes has drawn attention to the important role of the Williamite movement through the early 19th century when many thousands of Orangemen were enrolled in English and Irish lodges while their Grand Master, another Duke of Cumberland, eighth son of George III, schemed to retain the united throne of Britain and Hanover for the Brunswick family (Victoria, as a woman, being ineligible for the Hanoverian sovereignty). The scheme failed, of course, many Orangemen were disillusioned and even their Williamite glasses have become surprisingly rare.

The *privateer ship* undertaking licensed piracy was another popular theme associated with mid-Georgian days (and Victorian copyists). Privateer glasses in Bedford's Cecil Higgins Museum, for example, wish success to the frigate *Eagle* under Captain Dibdin and under Captain Knill (both known to have sailed her from Bristol in 1757). Admiral Rodney is surprisingly rare on glasses; Admiral Byng, shot for now-questioned cowardice, is recalled inaccurately by a figure hanged from a yard-arm.

Nelson glasses of all vintages abound including pairs of goblets one engraved with the *Victory* and the other with his funeral catafalque. Some bear the name LORD NELSON in a wreath; some are rimmed with the names of the Admirals Nelson, Duncan, St Vincent and Howe, or cite the naval battles that preceded Trafalgar. *Wellington* commemoratives include the popular glass declaring LD WELLINGTON FOR EVER with sword of war and dove of peace. More commemorative glasses belong to the 19th century including those engraved with rose, thistle and shamrock to celebrate the Union of Great Britain and Ireland, 1 January 1801.

A picturesque glass in the late Georgian romantic manner is associated with George IV's coronation, 1821. This recalls a medieval custom, showing the King's Champion, mounted and in armour, holding up a glove or a goblet. But many more vessels are associated with unknown men enjoying themselves, their glasses declaring their allegiance to their regiment, perhaps or one of the 'home guard' Volunteer units of Napoleonic times, or to a trade association, or the Oddfellows or Freemasonry. Many sturdy tumblers were engraved with set-squares, dividers, entwined triangles, pillars, sun, moon and stars, fraternal inscriptions, or even a curious little prone figure of Solomon, but even with such familiar Masonic symbols the collector goes warily. Some examples, of course, are merely rough modern etchings and more, it has been suggested, belong to other Georgian 'lodges' unconnected with Freemasonry.

Many inscriptions on glasses and decanters are self-explanatory such as those supporting Parliamentary election candidates, for example, or applauding John Wilkes, fiery champion of Liberty, these sometimes showing his release from the Tower as a bird singing above an open cage. References to the 'King and Constitution' may be associated with the *Reform Act*, 1832. But even a

93. Commemorative Nelson goblets with his funeral catafalque and
'H.M.S. *Victory*'.

seemingly obvious engraving may be somewhat misleading. The
huge single-span iron bridge over the Wear at Sunderland may be
inscribed with the year of its construction, 1796, but was endlessly
commemorated through the 1820s to 1840s. Vera Walker has
pointed out that the bridge was altered in 1859 when circular
struts were replaced by cross struts. The Laing Art Gallery and
Museum at Newcastle upon Tyne has a finely engraved goblet
showing the Chain Bridge at Scotswood, near Newcastle, opened
1831. Views of Newcastle's high-level bridge date no earlier than
Queen Victoria's opening of it in 1850. But by then the commemorative vessel might be a tankard with the scene pressed in
high relief.

94. Waisted tumbler
firing glass with very
thick base. Masonic
emblems among scrolls of
flowers and leaves in
yellow and white enamels.
1770s; height 5 ins.
Corning Museum of
Glass, New York.

119

CHAPTER FOURTEEN

Irish Glass

RELUCTANTLY we have to accept that Irish flint-glass decanters and drinking glasses are usually indistinguishable from contemporaneous English work. Equally unwelcome to some collectors is the fact that very many were made by Englishmen working in Ireland and in any case were only a relatively small part of the total produced in the British Isles, the Irish flint-glass factories being fewer than a quarter the number making decorative glass in England.

Hugh Wakefield has pointed out that in 1825 the Excise duty newly imposed on Irish flint-glass produced about £20,000 compared with rather more than £20,000 from Scotland and about £170,000 from England. Nevertheless, Irish glass has never lost the glamour associated by late-Georgian England with a region long regarded as remotely barbarous but then becoming the romantic Emerald Isle.

Among the myths that long surrounded the ware the notion of a blue tint or tinge peculiar to Ireland – or to Waterford – has long been dismissed. Throughout the boom period of Irish glass impurities in the ingredients usually imparted the faintest hint of dusky, variable 'colour' to any flint-glass, English or Irish, and inevitably decolorisers were applied with differing degrees of skill and success. A particular source of trouble was traced to the fine lead widely supplied to English and Irish glassmen from Derbyshire and obviously the thickness of the glass used for the deepest Irish cutting tended to emphasise any colour tinge. But in *c.* 1810 a Staffordshire firm improved the preparation of the Derbyshire lead that they supplied to all major glasshouses. Subsequently in both countries the best glass was more brilliantly clear, especially of course when old glass (cullet) was omitted from the melting pots and the tale glass skimmed from the top of the pots was set aside.

London, Stourbridge, Birmingham, Sunderland and Bristol

120

were then producing comparable glass and this was cut with the same skills in many indistinguishable patterns. But all this imparts a particular appeal to such glass as can fairly be attributed to the Irish houses, including some magnificent work. For the rest, the term Anglo-Irish is a sensible compromise.

So far as decanters and drinking glasses are concerned this leaves only a comparatively small amount of undisputed Irish glass and scarcely any drinking glasses—not even the fluted bucket-bowl goblets undoubtedly popular with Irish makers. However a few workaday decanters and still fewer water jugs part-moulded by the mould-blown technique show their makers' names in relief somewhat illegibly on their bases, though even here some clearly defined names are modern work.

Among ornamental details the collector assumes an Irish (probably Cork) origin for vessels cut or engraved around the body with the vesica pattern, consisting of stars or sprigs alternating with horizontal pointed ovals formed from parts of intersecting circles. Doubtless an Irish origin may be assumed too for many of the decanters and drinking glasses engraved with rose, thistle and especially flourishing shamrock or with three-loop bows, that commemorated the Union of Britain and Ireland, 1801.

Deep-cut diamond patterns were used by all the English and Irish glass-cutters, but common sense suggests that luxury Irish glass, untaxed until 1825, is more likely than its English counterpart to show the deepest cutting in the most extravagantly heavy glass, such as horizontal step cutting on jug and decanter shoulders c. 1820 and the thick vertical reeding or 'pillar flutes' that followed. By then England as well as Ireland and indeed all western Europe shared a liking for vertical ornament.

For the rest, Irish decanters from the 1780s to 1790s, like the English, showed a return to finger-aiding neck-rings and a gradual change from the vertical disc stopper to the horizontal mushroom shape. This might be cut, but was far more often mould-pinched with radiating grooves and frequently raised well above the decanter's brim by a straight or ball-knopped stem, a detail too narrowly ascribed to glass from Waterford or Cork.

The whole history of Irish glass shows close links with English work. There are occasional medieval references to the craft and enough glass was made under Elizabethan and early Stuart

95. A suggestion of the vesica pattern among the large diamonds cut in relief all over two attractive tumblers of *c.* 1800; height 5 ins and 4 ins.
Corning Museum of Glass, New York.

privilege to make tree-felling for furnaces prohibited in 1641. Dublin had a glasshouse as early as 1675 and the familiar Round Glasshouse was established in the 1690s–advertising in the 1740s and 1750s as the only flint-glass manufactury. In 1752 their 'newest fashion' vessels included 'drinking glasses, water bottles, claret and burgundy ditto, decanters, jugs, water glasses' as well as a range of dessert glasses. Cut and flowered glasses were specified 'of any kind of pattern, viz:- wine glasses with a vine border, toasts or any flourish whatever, beer ditto with same . . .'. But it closed in 1755 and disappointingly the well-known letter-writer Mrs Delany commented in 1759 from Delville: 'I send to England for good glass'.

Among notable Dublin glassmakers, a British company under Richard Williams was at work from *c.* 1764–advertising in 1770 'all the newest fashioned enamelled, flowered, cut and plain wine, beer and cyder glasses, common wines and drams, rummers, decanters . . .'. The firm was subsidised by the Dublin Society and, as techniques and tools improved in Ireland as in England, made great quantities of deeply cut table glass during the early 19th century until it closed in 1829.

This indeed was a typical story of Irish glass. Ireland had been excluded from England's early success in flint-glass. Their glass-men were omitted from the Excise Acts that increasingly taxed the English manufacturers, but also were prohibited from exporting to England. Complete freedom to trade worldwide came in 1780 as an indirect result of the American war but subjection to Excise duty-by-weight only followed in 1825. By the mid 1780s glass-houses were at work in Belfast, Dublin, Waterford, Cork and Newry. For nearly fifty golden years Ireland could manufacture increasingly massive, deeply cut wares in the styles most favoured by English and American customers and aided by the English manufacturers who, with skilled craftsmen, hastened to take advantage of this tax freedom. Most of the free-blown cut glass went to America while cheaper mould-blown vessels undersold English work in England.

Undoubtedly the tax imposition in 1825 affected Irish production, but in any case by then tastes were beginning to change and soon were influenced drastically by the vast development of America's cheap press-patterned, pseudo deeply cut glass.

To complete the Dublin story, little is known of a number of the Dublin flint-glass makers and the somewhat dusky glass never won the reputation for brilliant clarity enjoyed by Waterford. Much was coloured, rich blue, green and amber and frequently blown to shape with the aid of part-moulds.

Names of Dublin firms are found occasionally on the bases of such decanters. These appear somewhat illegibly in relief lettering, having been included in the mould shaping of the vessels' lower bodies: they are unclear because produced by blowing the molten glass rather than pressing it, as explained in Chapter Four. But these are mainly names of wholesalers or retailers, such as ARM-STRONG, ORMOND QUAY; MARY CARTER & SON; and FRANCIS COLLINS. Charles Mulvany (mark C M Co) is known to have been a manu-facturer as well as a retailer and J. D. Ayckbower or Ayckboum, a glasscutter from London and Bath, made glass briefly c. 1800. The important researcher into Irish glass, M. S. Dudley Westropp, recorded also the firm of Chebsey & Co., Venice Glasshouse, Dublin, highly successful from c. 1787 but terminated by Thomas Chebsey's death in 1798. A glasshouse was at work in Dublin, c. 1855 to 1895, run by the brothers Thomas and John Pugh, whose

96. Decanter bases showing how names were introduced in the mould-blown pattern (darkened for photographing). Collins was a merchant, selling, for example, mould-blown glass from Belfast.

father came from a glasshouse in Stourbridge (by Thomas with his son Richard from *c.* 1860). They shared in the current fashion for highly skilled ornament by Bohemian engravers and the National Museum, Dublin, has fine examples such as an engraved tumbler and cut and engraved commemorative goblet.

In Belfast another Englishman, Benjamin Edwards from Bristol, after a brief spell in Drumrea, began making glass in 1776. In 1781 he advertised that he had brought a glass-cutter from England and made cut and plain decanters, punch glasses, goblets and the like. He retired in 1807, but the firm was continued by his son until 1826. The mould-blown mark was B EDWARDS BELFAST, typically found on slender pear-shaped, narrow-lipped decanters. These might have two neck-rings above long shoulder facets as well as the usual moulded fluting above the base, some being lightly patterned with such motifs as pendant swags. Dudley Westropp, tracing the Belfast story, noted that flint-glass manufacture ended there in 1868.

Waterford, however, has always been first favourite with collectors. Here glass was made 1729 to 1740, but the 'founder of Anglo-Irish glass', yet another Englishman, was John Hill, son of a Stourbridge industrialist and glassmaker. Hill brought with him from England some 60 workmen skilled in all parts of the craft as well as formulae, designs and a genius for organisation when he became works manager at the glasshouse built by the merchant brothers George and William Penrose in 1783. From 1786 control

97. Decanters showing the gentle undulations of mould-blown work. The three with the vesica pattern are marked CORK GLASS CO.

passed to another Englishman, Jonathan Gatchell and the works flourished, employing as many as 200 craftsmen; in one two-year period over 100,000 drinking glasses were despatched to New York. But Gatchell died in 1823 and although his family continued the firm its output fell. Much magnificent glass was produced in the 19th century; however, even a massive display at the 1851 Great Exhibition could not revive the falling sales. This included quart and pint decanters cut from top to base in hollow prisms and massive pillars, described as 'in the German style' but dwarfed by still larger items.

Dudley Westropp in his book *Irish Glass* notes that the Waterford records refer to drinking glasses by such names as Regents, Nelsons, Masons (firing glasses), rummers, hob-nobs, flutes, drams, thumbs and dandies (small tumblers holding a quarter-pint). He illustrates a number of drawings that belonged to the foreman-cutter Samuel Miller. These include decanters, wine glasses and tumblers of *c.* 1830, the decanters straight-sided in the fashion of their day, mainly with heavy horizontal or vertical cutting, occasionally with printies and interesting curves. Notes with the patterns include references mainly to splits, round flutes, stuck flutes, 'new star at bottom'. Notes to the wine glasses refer for example to one glass with '5 arches round, new star bottom, 24 points'. Another had 'broad and narrow shell flutes, 4 of each, cut shanks and stands'.

Prussian shape decanters mould-blown with the name PENROSE

WATERFORD show wide flat mouth brims and the usual triple neck-rings and fluting below minor engraving such as curves arched between vertical panels or pendant loops between sprigs, often emphasised by fillings of cross-hatching to form areas of small diamonds. It must be realised, of course, that the process that permitted manufacturers' marks was intended to serve the mass market and bears no relation to the firms' cost-regardless free-blown work.

This must also be remembered when noting decanters from Cork, mould-blown with the names of CORK GLASS Co. and WATER-LOO Co. CORK. As in Waterford, glassmaking began in Cork in the early 1780s, the proprietors claiming English know-how. The Cork Glass Company's mould-marked decanters tend to be long-necked slender vessels with herringbone markings on their neck-rings and peculiarly flat mushroom stoppers. Cutters and engravers favoured the vesica pattern, the ovals often filled with stars.

The Waterloo Glass House Company, launched 1815, also tends to be judged by the limited representation of its mould-marked decanters. These, in Prussian shape, relied for design and ornament on Waterford and the Cork Glass Company, with a similar circle of scale pattern or sprigs below the triple neck-rings and with stars, pendant loops and variants of the vesica engraved above the customary shallow moulded fluting. The company's proprietor, Daniel Foley, advertised that it employed 100 workmen making a wide range of table wares but he retired in 1830 and the works appears to have closed in 1835.

A third Cork factory, the Terrace Glass Works, operated from 1818 under E. & R. Ronayne, still employing about forty glass-cutters in the late 1830s, but closed in 1841.

Flint-glass was also made in Newry, Co. Armagh, in the late 18th century and again in the 1820s to 1840s. And it is known that other establishments shared those splendid years by specialising in the separate craft of glass-cutting, in Cork and elsewhere, working on plain glass vessels supplied by local factories. But what, one may wonder, happened to Daniel Foley's new musical band with glass instruments, 'serpents, horns, trumpets, etc.' advertised in 1816, or his glass net 'which when seen will astonish the world'?

Index

N.B.: Page numbers in *italic* refer to illustrations

ACKNOWLEDGEMENTS

Photographs
Broadfield House Glass Museum, Kingswinford
35; Brooklyn Museum, New York 10, 50;
Christie Manson and Woods, London 15;
Corning Museum of Glass, New York 43, 51,
53, 89, 91, 94, 95; Cumbria Crystal 25, 87;
Delomosne & Son, London 1, 2, 14, 17, 19, 29,
30, 32, 33, 34, 42, 45, 46, 47, 48, 50, 52, 55, 56,
57, 58, 62, 66, 86, 93, 97; Hamlyn Group
Picture Library frontispiece, 11, 23, 31, 74, 80,

81; Hamlyn Group – Sidney Darby and Son,
West Bromwich 3, 8, 36, 37, 38, 83, 84, 85;
Hamlyn Group – Guest, Gidden and
Stanisstreet, Brierley Hill 4, 7, 20, 26, 27, 28, 41,
59, 71, 73, 78, 79; Pilkington Brothers, St
Helens 6; Spink and Son, London 61; Stuart and
Sons, Stourbridge 82; Victoria and Albert
Museum, London 5, 9, 12, 13, 18, 21, 22, 39,
40, 44, 75, 76, 77, 88.